GRADE 4

S0-AYD-282

100 Math Practice Pages

New York • Toronto • London • Auckland • Sydney
Mexico City • New Delhi • Hong Kong • Buenos Aires **Teaching** *Resources*

Edited by Mela Ottaiano
Cover design by Lindsey Dekker
Interior design by Melinda Belter

ISBN: 978-0-545-79940-9
Copyright © 2015 by Scholastic Inc., Betsy Franco, Matt Friedman, Christine Hood, Bob Krech and Joan Novelli,
Jan Meyer, Judith A. Muschla and Gary Robert Muschla, Liane B. Onish
Illustrations copyright © by Scholastic Inc.
All rights reserved.
Published by Scholastic Inc.
Printed in the U.S.A.

1 2 3 4 5 6 7 8 9 10   40   22 21 20 19 18 17 16 15

Contents

Introduction

In today's busy classrooms, it is vital to maximize learning time. That's where *100 Math Practice Pages, Grade 4* comes in. The activities in this book are designed to review and reinforce a range of math skills and concepts students will build throughout the year. Each page provides focused, individual practice on an essential, grade-level skill students are expected to master, including place value, addition, subtraction, multiplication, division, fractions, decimals, measurement, geometry, and data analysis.

Reviewing concepts students have already learned is a good way to keep their math skills sharp and to discover where revisiting a skill may be beneficial. You know your students best, so feel free to pick and choose among the activities, and incorporate those as you see fit. The goal is to build automaticity, fluency, and accuracy so students succeed in school.

How to Use This Book

Preview each activity page to ensure that students have the skills needed to complete it. If necessary, walk through its features with your class to provide an overview before you assign it and to make sure students understand the directions. Work out a model problem or two as a class.

The 100 practice pages can be used to enhance the curriculum during math time, to keep fast finishers on task anytime, or to assign as homework.

You'll find an answer key beginning on page 107. If time allows, you might want to review answers with the whole class. This approach provides opportunities for discussion, comparison, extension, reinforcement, and correlation to other skills and lessons. Your observations can direct the kinds of review or reinforcement you may want to add to your lessons. Alternatively, you may find that having students discuss activity solutions and strategies in small groups is another effective way to deepen understanding.

> The engaging activity pages are a great way to help students:
>
> ✓ reinforce key academic skills and concepts
>
> ✓ meet curriculum standards
>
> ✓ prepare for standardized tests
>
> ✓ succeed in school
>
> ✓ become lifelong learners

Meeting the Standards

Completing the exercises will help students meet the College and Career Readiness Standards for Mathematics, which serve as the backbone for the practice pages in this book. These broad standards were developed to establish a framework of clear educational expectations meant to provide students nationwide with a quality education that prepares them for college and careers. The following list details how the activities in this book align with the standards in the key areas of focus for students in grade 4.

Standards for Mathematics

MATHEMATICAL PRACTICE

1. Make sense of problems and persevere in solving them.

2. Reason abstractly and quantitatively.

3. Construct viable arguments and critique the reasoning of others.

4. Model with mathematics.

5. Use appropriate tools strategically.

6. Attend to precision.

7. Look for and make use of structure.

8. Look for and express regularity in repeating reasoning.

MATHEMATICAL CONTENT

✓ Operations and Algebraic Thinking

✓ Number and Operations in Base Ten

✓ Number and Operations—Fractions

✓ Measurement and Data

✓ Geometry

Name _____ Date _____

Order in the Court!

Now that we have your attention, put your skills at comparing and ordering numbers to the test. Solve three problems in a row to get Tic-Tac-Math!

Fill in the box with >, <, or =.

27 ☐ 48

Fill in the box with >, <, or =.

298 ☐ 289

Fill in the box with >, <, or =.

731 ☐ 665

Fill in the box with >, <, or =.

4,256 ☐ 4,256

Fill in the box with >, <, or =.

58,132 ☐ 57,215

Fill in the box with >, <, or =.

72,340 ☐ 73,101

Order these numbers from least to greatest:

____ 5,872

____ 5,725

____ 4,582

____ 5,820

Order these numbers from least to greatest:

____ 31,201

____ 38,562

____ 30,458

____ 32,000

____ 31,008

Order these numbers from least to greatest:

____ 567,890

____ 567,980

____ 560,987

____ 567,089

____ 567,098

100 Math Practice Pages, Grade 4 © 2015 • Scholastic Teaching Resources

Name _____ Date _____

Greater Than or Less Than?

Compare. Write <, =, or >.

1. 20,999 _____ 29,000

2. 15,551 _____ 15,155

3. 9,988 _____ 10,000

4. 90,404 _____ 91,777

5. 200,999 _____ 209,000

6. 150,551 _____ 150,155

7. 90,988 _____ 100,000

8. 908,444 _____ 901,888

9. 6,678 _____ sixty-six thousand seventy-eight

10. forty-five thousand three hundred _____ 45,300

11. 60,778 _____ sixty thousand seven hundred eighty-five

12. four hundred fifty thousand _____ 405,000

100 Math Practice Pages, Grade 4 © 2015 • Scholastic Teaching Resources

Name _____ Date _____

Cross-Number Puzzle

Here's a chance to practice your place-value skills. Fill in the numbers that match the place-value definitions. Read each puzzle clue carefully.

Hint
The place value clues may not go in order from highest to lowest place.

Across

b. seven hundreds, five tens, and six ones

c. three thousands, nine tens, zero hundreds, and nine ones

f. sixty thousands, two tens, seven ones, and five hundreds

g. six hundreds, seven thousands, two tens, and nine ones

h. zero ones, five hundreds, and one ten

i. five hundreds, seven tens, and eight ones

k. zero hundreds, two ones, six tens, and five thousands

Down

a. nine ones and eight tens

b. seven thousands, three hundreds, four tens, and five ones

c. nine ones, three hundreds, and two tens

d. nine hundreds, six tens, and zero ones

e. two hundreds, eight ones, six tens, and one thousand

g. seventy thousands, four ones, eight hundreds, and six tens

j. zero ones, zero hundreds, seven thousands, and seven tens

Name _____ Date _____

Number Place

Write the place value of the underlined digit.

1 4,5<u>6</u>7	**7** 1<u>2</u>,280
2 9,<u>3</u>56	**8** <u>9</u>3,518
3 <u>4</u>4,212	**9** 82,<u>6</u>94
4 <u>1</u>,849	**10** 7,4<u>6</u>1
5 2<u>1</u>2,873	**11** <u>1</u>01,605
6 50,21<u>5</u>	**12** 2<u>0</u>1,950

Name _____ Date _____

The Rounding Hound

Help the rounding hound sniff out the
right answers. Solve three problems
in a row to get Tic-Tac-Math!

Round 82 to the nearest ten.	Round 36 to the nearest ten.	Round 65 to the nearest ten.
Round 439 to the nearest hundred.	Round 288 to the nearest hundred.	Round 749 to the nearest hundred.
Round 5,295 to the nearest thousand.	Round 87,401 to the nearest ten thousand.	Round 35,576 to the nearest ten.

Rounding Rodeo

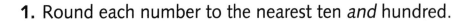

Complete each set of problems below.

1. Round each number to the nearest ten *and* hundred.

NUMBER	NEAREST 10	NEAREST 100
617		
1,862		
4,345		
89,083		

2. Round each number to its greatest place.

1,488 _____   435,456 _____

12,861 _____   922 _____

86,001 _____   277,005 _____

3. Round to the place of the underlined digit.

<u>9</u>31,488 _____   <u>4</u>35,465 _____

192,8<u>6</u>6 _____   922,<u>0</u>07 _____

8<u>0</u>6,001 _____   2<u>3</u>7,400 _____

Name _____ Date _____

What dessert do fish serve at their parties?

Add.

Solve the riddle using your answers.

574 +268 C	176 +117 N	478 +291 K	279 +246 B	317 +319 R	574 +397 T
318 +219 E	179 +149 A	285 +165 S	416 +376 P	195 +192 J	236 +378 F

Solve the Riddle! Write the letter that goes with each number.

___ ___ ___ ___   ___ ___ ___ ___ ___
842 636 328 525   842 328 769 537 450

100 *Math Practice Pages, Grade 4* © 2015 • Scholastic Teaching Resources

Addition Magician

Can you pull the answers to these problems out of your hat? Solve three addition problems in a row to get Tic-Tac-Math!

724 + 335	576 + 521	825 + 374
6,348 + 2,557	7,284 + 4,509	5,792 + 4,319
426 209 + 647	9,084 3,275 + 8,998	7,855 679 + 2,431

Name _____ Date _____

Add It Up!

Complete each set of problems below.

1. Add. Find the sum of the greatest and least answers.

6,016 + 4,410 = _____   240 + 807 = _____

249 + 370 = _____   1,209 + 7,005 = _____

4,254 + 1,709 = _____   156 + 918 = _____

_____ + _____ = _____

2. Add. Circle any answer that is an even number.

1,742	35,128	60,128
+ 7,065	+ 58,235	+ 11,234

305,549	3,122	239,127
+ 188,032	+ 6,239	+ 452,731

Name _____ Date _____

What does the wig say when he gets home?

Subtract.

Solve the riddle using your answers.

532	642	423	731	653	913
− 134	− 379	− 238	− 257	− 397	− 266
O	N	E	L	D	Y

924	656	831	936	721	842
− 185	− 158	− 299	− 777	− 395	− 277
I	A	H	M	R	U

Solve the Riddle!   Write the letter that goes with each number.

___ ___ ___ ___ ___ ___ ___ ,
532 739   532 398 263 185 647

___ ___ ___ ___ ___ ___ .
739 159   532 498 739 326

Name _____ Date _____

Subtraction Action

Want to earn a part in our new subtraction movie? Solve three subtraction problems in a row to get Tic-Tac-Math!

755 − 246	592 − 383	853 − 160
302 − 116	607 − 239	503 − 345
7,485 − 5,918	1,092 − 835	8,452 − 7,693

100 Math Practice Pages, Grade 4 © 2015 • Scholastic Teaching Resources

Super Subtraction

Subtract.

1		7	
	7,464 − 3,127		838 − 657

2		8	
	657 − 294		6,345 − 5,812

3		9	
	5,738 − 4,266		9,816 − 7,425

4		10	
	74,226 − 33,281		8,038 − 697

5		11	
	65,721 − 20,408		69,249 − 5,872

6		12	
	5,784 − 4,669		90,896 − 2,628

Name _____ Date _____

The Great Outdoors

Solve each word problem. Show your work in the tank.

1. A scientist found 84 dinosaur eggs in one location and 201 in another location. She had expected to find 300 eggs. By how much did she miss her goal?

_____

2. Captain Karl has 32 sailboats and 27 rowboats to rent. Today he rented 46 boats. How many boats were *not* rented?

_____

Name _____ Date _____

Comparing Products

Solve each equation. Then write
<, >, or = in the box.

1

$$
\begin{array}{r} 6 \\ \times\ 5 \\ \hline \end{array}
\qquad
\begin{array}{r} 3 \\ \times\ 10 \\ \hline \end{array}
$$

2

$$
\begin{array}{r} 7 \\ \times\ 9 \\ \hline \end{array}
\qquad
\begin{array}{r} 11 \\ \times\ 6 \\ \hline \end{array}
$$

3

$$
\begin{array}{r} 6 \\ \times\ 7 \\ \hline \end{array}
\qquad
\begin{array}{r} 5 \\ \times\ 8 \\ \hline \end{array}
$$

4

$$
\begin{array}{r} 7 \\ \times\ 5 \\ \hline \end{array}
\qquad
\begin{array}{r} 6 \\ \times\ 6 \\ \hline \end{array}
$$

5

$$
\begin{array}{r} 5 \\ \times\ 5 \\ \hline \end{array}
\qquad
\begin{array}{r} 8 \\ \times\ 3 \\ \hline \end{array}
$$

6

$$
\begin{array}{r} 2 \\ \times\ 9 \\ \hline \end{array}
\qquad
\begin{array}{r} 6 \\ \times\ 3 \\ \hline \end{array}
$$

7

$$
\begin{array}{r} 7 \\ \times\ 2 \\ \hline \end{array}
\qquad
\begin{array}{r} 4 \\ \times\ 4 \\ \hline \end{array}
$$

8

$$
\begin{array}{r} 12 \\ \times\ 7 \\ \hline \end{array}
\qquad
\begin{array}{r} 9 \\ \times\ 9 \\ \hline \end{array}
$$

Mega-Multiplication

Flex your multiplication muscles.
Multiply using mental math.

1. 3 × 40 = _____

2. 5 × 70 = _____

3. 7 × 300 = _____

4. 4 × 50 = _____

5. 3 × 400 = _____

6. 8 × 600 = _____

7. 3 × 80 = _____

8. 5 × 600 = _____

9. 2 × 900 = _____

10. 6 × 30 = _____

11. 4 × 500 = _____

12. 6 × 700 = _____

13. 8 × 6,000 = _____

14. 4 × 7,000 = _____

15. 9 × 2,000 = _____

16. 6 × 4,000 = _____

17. 5 × 3,000 = _____

18. 7 × 8,000 = _____

19. 3 × 8,000 = _____

20. 8 × 9,000 = _____

21. 8 × 6,000 = _____

22. 9 × 9,000 = _____

23. 12 × 1,000 = _____

24. 10 × 10,000 = _____

Moo-ltiplication

Everyone knows cows are not good at multiplication.
Are you? Solve three problems in a row to get
Tic-Tac-Math!

$$
\begin{array}{r}
30 \\
\times\ 10 \\
\hline
\end{array}
\qquad
\begin{array}{r}
20 \\
\times\ 40 \\
\hline
\end{array}
\qquad
\begin{array}{r}
30 \\
\times\ 50 \\
\hline
\end{array}
$$

$$
\begin{array}{r}
23 \\
\times\ 20 \\
\hline
\end{array}
\qquad
\begin{array}{r}
31 \\
\times\ 10 \\
\hline
\end{array}
\qquad
\begin{array}{r}
40 \\
\times\ 18 \\
\hline
\end{array}
$$

$$
\begin{array}{r}
45 \\
\times\ 26 \\
\hline
\end{array}
\qquad
\begin{array}{r}
81 \\
\times\ 93 \\
\hline
\end{array}
\qquad
\begin{array}{r}
79 \\
\times\ 48 \\
\hline
\end{array}
$$

Name _____ Date _____

Broadway Show

Fill in words and numbers as directed.
Then solve the problem.

Our class went to see a Broadway show. There were

_____ of us going, so we took a
(double-digit number)

_____ to get there. The ride
(mode of transportation)

there was very _____, but we made it on time.
(adjective)

The show was *Beauty and the* _____, starring
(noun)

_____ and _____. It was
(name of a famous person)   (name of a famous person)

so _____, it was definitely worth the price of the
(adjective)

tickets, which were _____ dollars each. We were
(double-digit number)

_____ all the way through the show. After, we
(verb ending in *-ing*)

went to a restaurant called The Lucky _____,
(noun)

which serves the traditional cuisine of _____.
(name of a place)

It was a really _____ night.
(adjective)

Solve This! How much did it cost for the
class to see the Broadway show? _____

Name _____ Date _____

Multiplier the Magnificent

Complete each set of problems below.

1. Multiply. Circle the two products
   that have a sum of 925.

   5 × 36 = _____   4 × 98 = _____   4 × 397 = _____

   6 × 752 = _____   6 × 816 = _____   8 × 78 = _____

   3 × 622 = _____   7 × 43 = _____   5 × 671 = _____

2. Multiply. Circle the pair of products
   that have a sum of 5,100.

   ```
       33              23              42              48
     × 22            × 11            × 12            × 99
   ```

   ```
       64              75              62              44
     × 39            × 29            × 42            × 83
   ```

Legs and Toes

Read the problems and then use multiplication to answer the questions.

Hint

Be sure to read all of the
information carefully.

1. An owl has a total of 8 toes. How many toes do
   15 owls have? _____

2. A mosquito, like most insects, has 6 legs. How
   many legs do 160 mosquitoes have? _____

3. A hippo has 4 toes on each foot. How many toes
   does a hippo have in all? _____

4. A spider has 8 legs. How many legs do 141 spiders have?
   _____

5. An ostrich has a total of 4 toes. How many toes do
   20 ostriches have? _____

6. A porcupine has 5 toes on each of its front paws and
   4 toes on each of its back paws. How many toes does
   a porcupine have in all? _____

Bonus!   Which has more toes: 2 owls or 3 ostriches? _____

Name _____ Date _____

Tower Power

Look at the quotient at the top of each block tower.
Then solve the problems on the tower. Circle each
block that shows a problem that can be answered
correctly with the quotient.

12

$12\overline{)144}$

$5\overline{)60}$

$12\overline{)12}$

$11\overline{)132}$

$4\overline{)44}$

8

$3\overline{)24}$

$9\overline{)63}$

$4\overline{)36}$

$6\overline{)48}$

$12\overline{)84}$

4

$5\overline{)35}$

$8\overline{)32}$

$10\overline{)40}$

$12\overline{)48}$

$2\overline{)8}$

9

$9\overline{)81}$

$11\overline{)77}$

$8\overline{)72}$

$3\overline{)27}$

$12\overline{)108}$

7

$6\overline{)42}$

$7\overline{)49}$

$2\overline{)14}$

$8\overline{)64}$

$3\overline{)21}$

 100 Math Practice Pages, Grade 4 © 2015 • Scholastic Teaching Resources

Name _____ Date _____

Remember the Remainder!

Solve three division problems in a row to get
Tic-Tac-Math! Don't forget the remainder!

$2\overline{)17}$ $5\overline{)28}$ $9\overline{)50}$

$3\overline{)28}$ $4\overline{)35}$ $7\overline{)51}$

$7\overline{)67}$ $8\overline{)34}$ $10\overline{)78}$

100 Math Practice Pages, Grade 4 © 2015 • Scholastic Teaching Resources

Division Design

Solve each division problem. Then use the key and color the design.

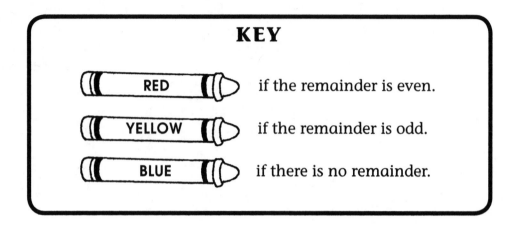

KEY

RED — if the remainder is even.

YELLOW — if the remainder is odd.

BLUE — if there is no remainder.

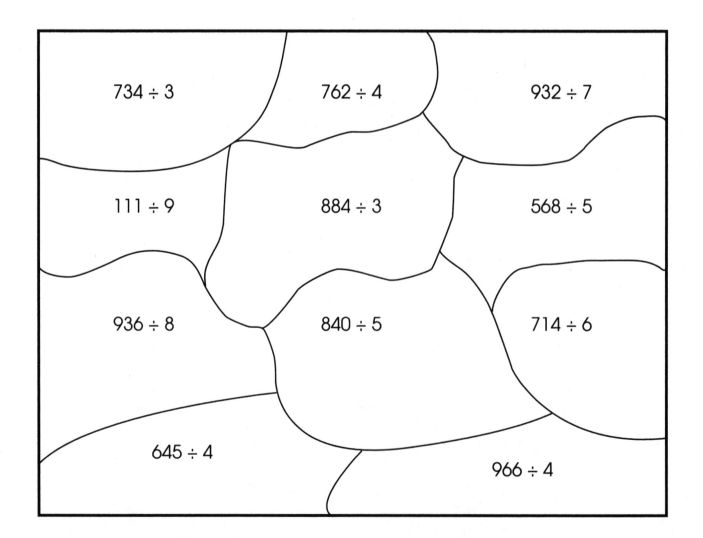

$734 \div 3$

$762 \div 4$

$932 \div 7$

$111 \div 9$

$884 \div 3$

$568 \div 5$

$936 \div 8$

$840 \div 5$

$714 \div 6$

$645 \div 4$

$966 \div 4$

Cool Quotients

Who knew division could be so cool! Solve three
division problems to get Tic-Tac-Math!

$3 \overline{)63}$ $2 \overline{)84}$ $9 \overline{)99}$

$4 \overline{)144}$ $8 \overline{)656}$ $7 \overline{)371}$

$4 \overline{)768}$ $3 \overline{)534}$ $9 \overline{)828}$

   100 Math Practice Pages, Grade 4 © 2015 • Scholastic Teaching Resources

Quick Quotients

Use number sense to estimate each quotient.

1 $37 \div 8 = $ _____	**10** $624 \div 9 = $ _____
2 $29 \div 4 = $ _____	**11** $34 \div 9 = $ _____
3 $155 \div 4 = $ _____	**12** $428 \div 6 = $ _____
4 $429 \div 7 = $ _____	**13** $650 \div 8 = $ _____
5 $493 \div 5 = $ _____	**14** $389 \div 8 = $ _____
6 $173 \div 3 = $ _____	**15** $6{,}341 \div 9 = $ _____
7 $314 \div 6 = $ _____	**16** $3{,}572 \div 4 = $ _____
8 $2{,}439 \div 6 = $ _____	**17** $4{,}166 \div 7 = $ _____
9 $3{,}177 \div 8 = $ _____	**18** $3{,}583 \div 5 = $ _____

100 Math Practice Pages, Grade 4 © 2015 • Scholastic Teaching Resources

Coins From Another Planet

Fill in words and numbers as directed.
Then solve the problem.

My Uncle _____
(first name of a boy)

collects coins from everywhere. He has them from

_____, _____, and even
(name of a place)   (name of a place)

_____. However, he just got his most valuable coins ever.
(name of a place)

They are from Planet _____ _____.
(adjective)   (noun)

In fact, he got 200 coins from there. He will donate them equally

to _____ museums. The coins are very
(choose a number: 10, 20, 25, or 50)

_____. A picture of _____ is on one
(adjective)   (first and last name of a boy or girl)

side. The other side shows the planet's _____. Each coin
(noun)

is worth about _____ _____. Wow!
(number greater than 1)   (money unit, plural)

Solve This! How many coins will
each museum get? _____

Name _____

Date _____

Division Diner

Solve each word problem.
Show your work in the tank.

1. At Dinah's Diner, they serve 300 ounces of milk every day. The milk comes in 12-ounce glasses. How many glasses of milk do people order?

_____

2. During the lunch rush, the chef cooks 810 French fries. If 18 fries come with each serving, how many servings of French fries do people order?

_____

Times to Divide

**Should you multiply or divide? Find out when you solve
three word problems in a row to get Tic-Tac-Math!**

Three friends split a $15 meal. If each pays the same amount, how much does each friend owe?	Alex, Manny, Derek, and Barry each owns 8 baseball cards. How many cards do they have in all?	Pop buys 9 packs of gum with 5 sticks of gum in each pack. How many sticks of gum does Pop have in all?
Annie has 84 stickers. She keeps an equal number of stickers on each of 7 pages in her sticker book. How many stickers are on each page?	Barry spent 17 minutes on his writing homework. He spent 3 times as long on his math homework. How long did Barry spend on math homework?	There are 72 cookies in a box. Inside the box are 3 wrapped sleeves, each with an equal number of cookies in it. How many cookies are in each sleeve?
Britt is saving up to buy a $252 video-game system. If she saves $6 per week, how long will she need to save?	Conrad is counting down hours until his birthday, which is exactly 21 days from now. There are 24 hours in a day. How many hours away is Conrad's birthday?	If a car could drive 54 miles per hour for 218 hours, how far could it travel?

Magic Show

**Fill in words and numbers as directed.
Then solve the problem.**

_____ the Great does a magic
(name of a girl)

show that is simply _____.
(adjective)

She performs _____
(number greater than 1)

tricks during her act. In one of her tricks, she

pulls ten _____ from her
(plural noun)

ear. That is _____! She also waves a wand and
(adjective)

makes _____ float! In her best trick, she pulls
(plural noun)

_____ _____ out of a hat. She
(choose a number: 10 or 20)   (plural noun)

does this _____ times in all. Then 10 lucky audience
(choose a number: 2, 5, or 10)

members get a special surprise. She divides everything she pulled from the hat

evenly among them.

How many items
from the hat does each
lucky audience member get? _____

Sports Math

Solve each word problem.
Show your work in the tank.

1. The Spring Town Arena holds 15,300 people. There are 3 levels and each level contains 60 sections. How many seats are in each section?

_____

2. Tonight's game and tomorrow's game at Spring Town Arena are sold out! If a ticket to the game costs $11, how much money in total did fans pay to see the two games?

_____

Name _____ Date _____

Roxie's Front-End Repairs

Missing the front end of an arithmetic problem? Go to Roxie's. She has the best front-end repair shop in town! Look in Roxie's box of spare parts for the correct front end for each of these equations. When you find it, write it on the line in front of the problem where it belongs. Be careful, though. You won't need all of Roxie's spare parts.

1. _____ 8 = 40

2. _____ 11 = 22

3. _____ 3 = 27

4. _____ 8 = 20

5. _____ 6 = 23

6. _____ 12 = 27

7. _____ 3 = 21

8. _____ 6 = 24

9. _____ 15 = 21

10. _____ 6 = 36

SPARE PARTS

14 +

6 +

4 ×

31 +

17 +

8 ×

9 ×

39 −

26 −

5 ×

11 +

7 ×

23 +

6 ×

28 −

It's Too Much!

Dig up only the information you need to solve these problems. Solve three problems in a row to get Tic-Tac-Math!

At 6:00 P.M., Johnny bought a calculator for $4.95 and a protractor for $1.80. How much did Johnny spend in all?	During their fishing trip, Patty caught 5 fish. One of them weighed 15 pounds! Patty's sister caught twice as many fish. How many fish did Patty's sister catch?	There are 27 kids in Anabeth's class, 26 kids in Carlos's class, and 24 kids in Pete's class. How many more kids are in Carlos's class than in Pete's class?
Andrea's basketball team won their game 54 to 48. Andrea and Gail scored 24 of the team's points! If Gail scored 10 points, how many points did Andrea score?	Drake spent 28 minutes on 20 math problems, and 30 minutes writing 5 essays. How much longer did he spend on the essays than on the math problems?	A movie ticket costs 2 times as much as popcorn, and 3 times as much as a soda. If a movie costs $9.00, how much is popcorn?
In a football game, Dale scored 3 touchdowns and Jimmy scored 4. If a touchdown is worth 6 points, how many points did Jimmy score?	There are 15,000 people in Bigville. That's 2,000 more than are in Middleville, and 5,000 more than are in Littleville. How many people live in Littleville?	A 6-bedroom house in Homesburg costs $250,000 and a 4-bedroom house costs half as much. How much is a 4-bedroom house in Homesburg?

100 Math Practice Pages, Grade 4 © 2015 • Scholastic Teaching Resources

Name _____ Date _____

Body Facts

The human body is far more complicated than the most advanced machine. Use the body facts below to solve the problems.

1 The average baby's body has 350 bones. As a person gets older, some of these bones grow together. This is why the average adult has 206 bones.

What is the difference between the number of bones in the body of the average adult and the body of the average baby? _____

2 Doctors recommend that the average person should exercise at least 30 minutes every day.

How many minutes of exercise is this each week? _____

How many hours of exercise is this each week? _____

3 The average person has 650 muscles. Fourteen muscles are needed for smiling, but 43 muscles are needed for frowning.

How many muscles are not needed for frowning? _____

4 The average person breathes 20 times per minute during normal activity.

Based on this rate, how many breaths does the average person take each hour? _____

Each day? _____

5 The average person's heart beats 100,000 times per day.

How many beats is this per hour? _____
(Round answers to the nearest whole number.)

How many beats is this per minute? _____

Name _____ Date _____

Factor Hunt

Find all factor pairs for the following whole numbers.

1. What are the factor pairs of 18?

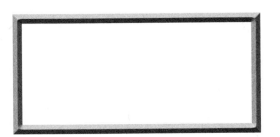

4. What are the factor pairs of 64?

2. What are the factor pairs of 24?

5. What are the factor pairs of 72?

3. What are the factor pairs of 52?

6. What are the factor pairs of 96?

Name _____ Date _____

Mapping Multiples

Complete the Venn diagrams.

1. Use numbers between 0 and 50. Write multiples of 3 in one part.
   Write multiples of 5 in the other part. Write multiples of both 3 and 5
   in the overlapping part.

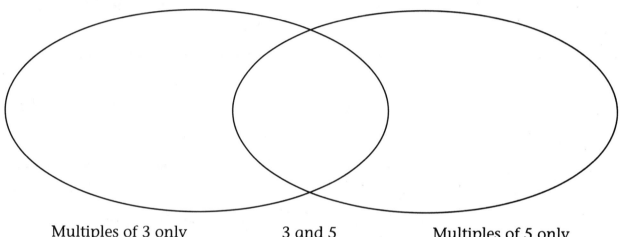

Multiples of 3 only   3 and 5   Multiples of 5 only

2. Use numbers between 0 and 50. Write multiples of 4 in one part.
   Write multiples of 6 in the other part. Write multiples of 4 and 6
   in the overlapping part.

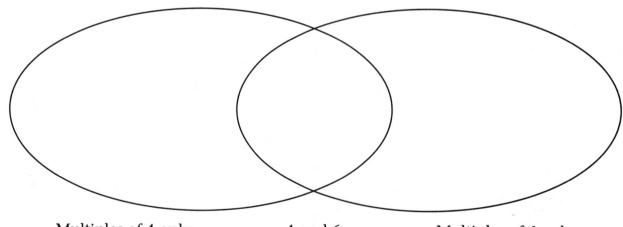

Multiples of 4 only   4 and 6   Multiples of 6 only

Name _____ Date _____

Do You See a Pattern?

There are several patterns here. Solve three problems in a row to get Tic-Tac-Math!

What's the next number in this pattern?

2, 4, 6, 8, _____

What's the next number in this pattern?

1, 4, 7, 10, _____

What's the next number in this pattern?

45, 40, 35, 30, _____

What are the next three numbers in this pattern?

18, 21, 20, 23, 22

_____, _____, _____

What are the next three numbers in this pattern?

135, 133, 129, 121

_____, _____, _____

What are the next three numbers in this pattern?

9,600, 8,800, 8,400, 8,200

_____, _____, _____

What's next in this pattern?

Saturday
Monday
Wednesday
Friday

_____

What's next in this pattern?

March 5
March 12
March 19
March 26

_____

What's next in this pattern?

5:10
5:24
5:38
5:52

_____

 100 Math Practice Pages, Grade 4 © 2015 • Scholastic Teaching Resources

Name _____ Date _____

Fill 'Em In

Can you figure out what's missing in each of these patterns of numbers, letters, and designs? Fill in what's missing.

1. ABC   BCD   _____   DEF   _____   FGH   GHI

2. 15   16   25   ____   35   36   45   46   ____   56   65   66

3. ▲   _____   ▲▲   ✖✖   ▲▲▲   ✖✖✖   _____   ✖✖✖✖

4. 99   88   77   ____   55   ____   33   22   11

5. a   c   e   g   i   ___   m   ___   q   s   u   w

6. ↓   →   ↑   ←   ↓   ___   ↑   ←   ↓   →   ___   ←

7. z   y   ___   w   v   u   ___   s   r   q   ___   o

8. A   Z   ___   Y   C   X   D   ___   E   V   ___   U   G

Bonus!   Make up your own pattern using numbers, letters, or designs.

_____

Name _____ Date _____

The First Dinosaur

Dinosaurs ruled Earth for about 180 million years, until they died out 65 million years ago. Many historians agree that an Englishwoman, Mary Mantell, discovered the first dinosaur bones in 1822. What was this dinosaur named?

Answer:

I __ __ __ __ __ __ __ __
1 2 3 4 5 6 7 8 9

Complete each pattern. Find the last answer of each pattern in the Answer Box, then write the letter of the answer in the space above its problem number. The first one has been done for you. **Hint:** Some letters will not be used.

1 1, 3, 5, 7, __9__ , __11__ , __13__

2 2, 4, 8, 16, _____ , _____ , _____

3 30, 29, 27, 24, _____ , _____ , _____

4 1, 6, 11, 16, _____ , _____ , _____

5 7, 8, 10, 13, _____ , _____ , _____

6 729, 243, 81, 27, _____ , _____ , _____

7 ●, ★, ●●, ★★, _____ , _____ , _____

8 ★●, ★★●, ★★●●, ★★★●●, _____ ,

   _____ , _____

9 ★, ★●, ★★, ★★●●, _____ ,

   _____ , _____

Answer Box

C. 14
S. ★★★★★
N. 28
R. 12
D. ●●●●
H. 192
A. 31
V. ★●★●★●
I. 13
U. 9
O. 1
N. ★★★★
G. 128
O. ★★★★●●●●
M. 22

The Great Gumball Machine

Fill in words and numbers as directed.
Then solve the problem.

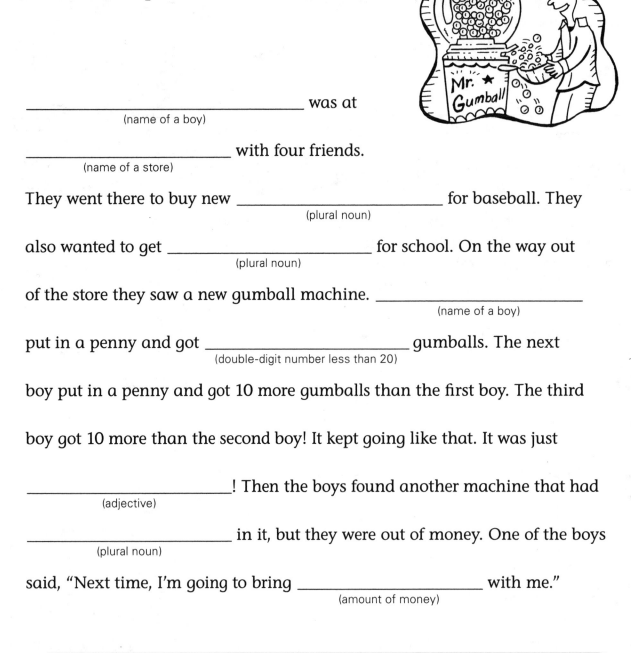

_____ was at
(name of a boy)

_____ with four friends.
(name of a store)

They went there to buy new _____ for baseball. They
(plural noun)

also wanted to get _____ for school. On the way out
(plural noun)

of the store they saw a new gumball machine. _____
(name of a boy)

put in a penny and got _____ gumballs. The next
(double-digit number less than 20)

boy put in a penny and got 10 more gumballs than the first boy. The third

boy got 10 more than the second boy! It kept going like that. It was just

_____! Then the boys found another machine that had
(adjective)

_____ in it, but they were out of money. One of the boys
(plural noun)

said, "Next time, I'm going to bring _____ with me."
(amount of money)

How many gumballs
did the fifth boy get? _____

Kid on a Grid

Jamaal just moved to a new town. This map shows the street corners where different places are located. Help Jamaal find his way around! Solve three coordinate-grid problems in a row to get Tic-Tac-Math!

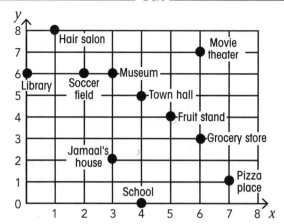

What is directly above the school on the map?

What is located at (2, 6)?

What is located at (5, 4)?

What are the coordinates of the hair salon?

What are the coordinates of the pizza place?

Which place has the same x-coordinate as the movie theater?

Jamaal rides his bike on the roads from the school to the library at a rate of one block per minute. If he stays on the roads on the grid and he doesn't backtrack, how long will the trip take him?

Jamaal's bike gets a flat tire, so he walks it home from the library. If he walks one block every five minutes and stays on the roads without back-tracking, how long will the walk take?

Jamaal's bike gets a flat tire, so he walks it home from the library. If he walks one block every five minutes and stays on the roads without backtracking, how long will the walk take?

A Big Group

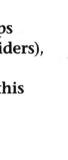

The largest of all animal groups includes insects, arachnids (spiders), and crustaceans (lobsters and shrimp). What is the name of this animal group?

Answer:

___ ___ ___ ___ ___ ___ ___ ___ ___ ___
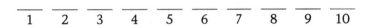
 1   2   3   4   5   6   7   8   9   10

To answer the question, match the equations with the properties they demonstrate. Write the letter of the property in the space above the equation number.

1 $7 \times 0 = 0$ _____

2 $(7 \times 3) \times 4 = 7 \times (3 \times 4)$ _____

3 $21 + 8 = 8 + 21$ _____

4 $10 \times 1 = 10$ _____

5 $(9 \times 6) \times 2 = 9 \times (6 \times 2)$ _____

6 $3 \times 5 = 5 \times 3$ _____

7 $(3 + 9) + 4 = 3 + (9 + 4)$ _____

8 $106 \times 4 = 4 \times 106$ _____

9 $12 + 0 = 12$ _____

10 $9 \times (4 + 8) = (9 \times 4) + (9 \times 8)$ _____

Properties

T. Commutative Property of Addition

P. Associative Property of Addition

D. Identity Property of Zero

O. Commutative Property of Multiplication

R. Associative Property of Multiplication

H. Identity Property of One

S. Distributive Property

A. Zero Property of Multiplication

Name _____ Date _____

Mystery Numbers

Write a number sentence.

Use _n_ for the unknown number.

Then solve.

1. The dividend is 54. The quotient is 9.

   What is the divisor? _____

2. The quotient is 129. The divisor is 3.

   What is the dividend? _____

3. The dividend is 126. The quotient is 3.

   What is the divisor? _____

4. The quotient is 66. The divisor is 9.

   What is the dividend? _____

5. The product is 1,950. One factor is 15.

   What is the other factor? _____

Name _____ Date _____

What's the Number?

Write a number sentence. Use *n* for
the unknown number. Then solve.
Hint: Read the problems carefully.

1 Add 435 to a number. The sum is 1,966.	**5** The product is 448. One factor is 7. What is the other factor?
2 Subtract a number from 625. The difference is 52.	**6** One factor is 151. The product is 1,812. What is the other factor?
3 The product is 0. One factor is 1,000. What is the other factor?	**7** The quotient is 11. The dividend is 396. What is the divisor?
4 The quotient is 64. The divisor is 48. What is the dividend?	**8** The dividend is 2,005. The quotient is 401. What is the divisor?

Sales Job

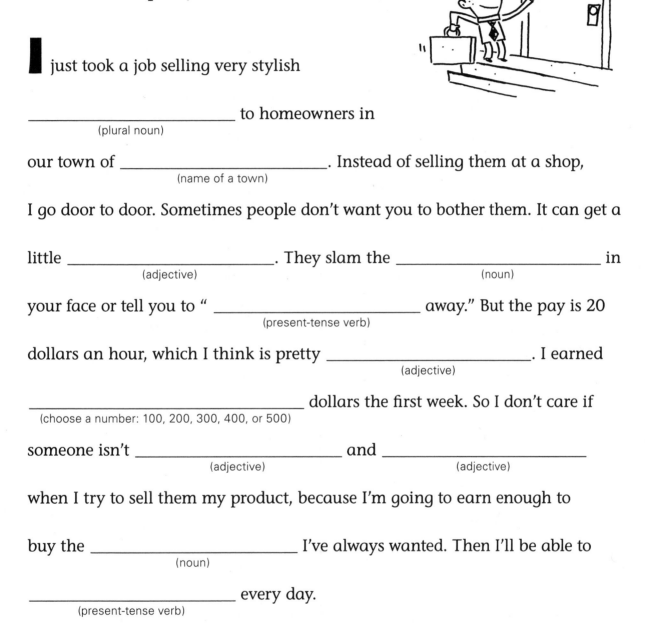

Fill in words and numbers as directed.
Then solve the problem.

I just took a job selling very stylish

_____ to homeowners in
　　　　(plural noun)

our town of _____. Instead of selling them at a shop,
　　　　　　　(name of a town)

I go door to door. Sometimes people don't want you to bother them. It can get a

little _____. They slam the _____ in
　　　　(adjective)　　　　　　　　　　　　　　　　　　　(noun)

your face or tell you to " _____ away." But the pay is 20
　　　　　　　　　　　(present-tense verb)

dollars an hour, which I think is pretty _____. I earned
　　　　　　　　　　　　　　　　　　　　　(adjective)

_____ dollars the first week. So I don't care if
(choose a number: 100, 200, 300, 400, or 500)

someone isn't _____ and _____
　　　　　　　(adjective)　　　　　　　　　　　　(adjective)

when I try to sell them my product, because I'm going to earn enough to

buy the _____ I've always wanted. Then I'll be able to
　　　　　(noun)

_____ every day.
　　(present-tense verb)

If *n* = the number of hours worked,
what is the value of *n* in this story? _____

Name _____   Date _____

What should you say to a blue heron?

Name the fraction of each shape that is shaded.

Solve the riddle using your answers.

 = _____
R

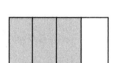 = _____
U

 = _____
C

 = _____
E

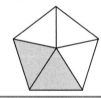 = _____
M

 = _____
N

 = _____
W

 = _____
H

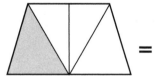 = _____
K

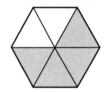 = _____
P

Solve the Riddle!   Write the letter that goes with each answer.

$\dfrac{1}{2}$ $\dfrac{7}{8}$ $\dfrac{5}{6}$ $\dfrac{5}{6}$ $\dfrac{1}{3}$ $\dfrac{3}{4}$ $\dfrac{4}{6}$ **!**

Name _____ Date _____

Meet the Slammers

Here is a picture of the Slammers, the best baseball team in the South Lakes junior league. This year, they won all but one of their games. Use the picture to answer these questions.

1. What fraction of the Slammers are wearing shirts with short sleeves? _____

2. What fraction of the Slammers are wearing glasses? _____

3. What fraction of the Slammers are standing? _____

4. What fraction of the Slammers are girls? _____

5. What fraction of the Slammers are boys? _____

6. What fraction of the girls have curly hair? _____

7. What fraction of the boys are wearing baseball caps. _____

8. What fraction of the boys who are wearing baseball caps are holding baseball bats? _____

Bonus! One-third of the Slammers have pet dogs at home. How many Slammers is that? _____

Name _____ Date _____

I'm $\frac{1}{2}$, But Call Me $\frac{2}{4}$

What's in a name? Well, if you're a fraction, you could have lots of names. Find out more when you solve three equivalent fraction problems in a row to get Tic-Tac-Math!

$\frac{1}{2} = \frac{}{4}$

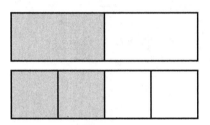

$\frac{2}{3} = \frac{}{6}$

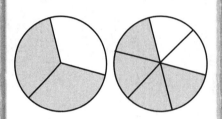

$\frac{3}{12} = \frac{}{8}$

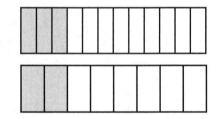

Are the fractions shown equivalent?

yes   no

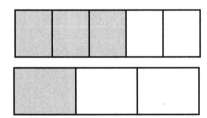

Are the fractions shown equivalent?

yes   no

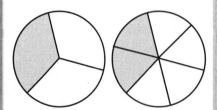

Are the fractions shown equivalent?

yes   no

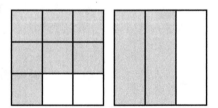

Circle any fraction that is equivalent to $\frac{2}{3}$.

$\frac{4}{5}$ $\frac{8}{12}$ $\frac{6}{8}$

Circle any fraction that is equivalent to $\frac{5}{9}$.

$\frac{45}{81}$ $\frac{25}{29}$

$\frac{48}{63}$ $\frac{20}{35}$

Circle any fraction that is equivalent to $\frac{12}{16}$.

$\frac{36}{40}$ $\frac{2}{9}$ $\frac{48}{54}$

$\frac{6}{8}$ $\frac{20}{25}$

Name _____ Date _____

Where do aliens wash?

Write the missing numerator.

Solve the riddle using your answers.

$$\frac{1}{2} = \frac{}{4} \quad M$$

$$\frac{2}{6} = \frac{}{9} \quad O$$

$$\frac{2}{3} = \frac{}{9} \quad S$$

$$\frac{1}{2} = \frac{}{8} \quad E$$

$$\frac{3}{4} = \frac{}{12} \quad A$$

$$\frac{1}{3} = \frac{}{15} \quad I$$

$$\frac{1}{2} = \frac{}{22} \quad H$$

$$\frac{1}{2} = \frac{}{16} \quad T$$

$$\frac{3}{10} = \frac{}{100} \quad R$$

$$\frac{2}{3} = \frac{}{18} \quad N$$

$$\frac{1}{2} = \frac{}{14} \quad G$$

$$\frac{1}{2} = \frac{}{20} \quad W$$

Solve the Riddle!   Write the letter that goes with each answer.

$$\overline{}_{5} \quad \overline{}_{12} \quad \overline{}_{2} \quad \overline{}_{4} \quad \overline{}_{8} \quad \overline{}_{4} \quad \overline{}_{3} \quad \overline{}_{30}$$

$$\overline{}_{6} \quad \overline{}_{11} \quad \overline{}_{3} \quad \overline{}_{10} \quad \overline{}_{4} \quad \overline{}_{30} \quad \overline{}_{6}$$

Ships Ahoy!

The longest canal in the world is in the Western Hemisphere. It is 2,400 feet long. What is the name of this canal?

Answer:

___ ___   ___ ___ ___ ___ ___ ___ ___ ___   ___ ___ ___ ___ ___ ___
6 10   5   4   3   1 12   8 14   2   16   7 13   9 15 11

To answer the question, match each fraction with an equivalent fraction in the Answer Box. Then write the letter of each equivalent fraction in the space above its problem number.

1 $\frac{9}{10}$ = _____

2 $\frac{4}{5}$ = _____

3 $\frac{2}{3}$ = _____

4 $\frac{4}{9}$ = _____

5 $\frac{3}{4}$ = _____

6 $\frac{2}{5}$ = _____

7 $\frac{5}{8}$ = _____

8 $\frac{1}{6}$ = _____

9 $\frac{3}{8}$ = _____

10 $\frac{6}{7}$ = _____

11 $\frac{5}{6}$ = _____

12 $\frac{5}{7}$ = _____

13 $\frac{5}{12}$ = _____

14 $\frac{1}{2}$ = _____

15 $\frac{7}{10}$ = _____

16 $\frac{7}{8}$ = _____

Answer Box

L. $\frac{15}{20}$ A. $\frac{12}{27}$

W. $\frac{12}{32}$ Y. $\frac{15}{18}$

T. $\frac{18}{21}$ N. $\frac{3}{18}$

E. $\frac{15}{24}$ S. $\frac{21}{24}$

W. $\frac{6}{9}$ E. $\frac{12}{15}$

A. $\frac{21}{30}$ E. $\frac{10}{14}$

A. $\frac{10}{24}$ S. $\frac{10}{25}$

R. $\frac{18}{20}$ C. $\frac{50}{100}$

Name _____ Date _____

Fractions—Made Simple

Fractions don't have to be so hard. In fact, they prefer to be simple. Solve three simplifying fraction problems in a row to get Tic-Tac-Math!

What is the greatest common factor of 6 and 8?	What is the greatest common factor of 4 and 12?	What is the greatest common factor of 15 and 25?
What is $\frac{6}{8}$ in simplest form?	What is $\frac{4}{12}$ in simplest form?	What is $\frac{15}{25}$ in simplest form?
What is $\frac{4}{18}$ in simplest form?	What is $\frac{12}{42}$ in simplest form?	What is $\frac{30}{75}$ in simplest form?

100 Math Practice Pages, Grade 4 © 2015 • Scholastic Teaching Resources

Name _____ Date _____

What do you call a dogcatcher?

Rename the fractions in lowest terms.

Solve the riddle using your answers.

$$\frac{3}{9} = \underline{\quad\quad}$$
S

$$\frac{15}{18} = \underline{\quad\quad}$$
R

$$\frac{15}{20} = \underline{\quad\quad}$$
V

$$\frac{14}{21} = \underline{\quad\quad}$$
O

$$\frac{14}{16} = \underline{\quad\quad}$$
E

$$\frac{6}{10} = \underline{\quad\quad}$$
L

$$\frac{4}{36} = \underline{\quad\quad}$$
T

$$\frac{14}{18} = \underline{\quad\quad}$$
B

$$\frac{21}{30} = \underline{\quad\quad}$$
C

$$\frac{3}{24} = \underline{\quad\quad}$$
M

$$\frac{4}{16} = \underline{\quad\quad}$$
P

$$\frac{10}{14} = \underline{\quad\quad}$$
A

Solve the Riddle! Write the letter that goes with each answer.

$$\frac{5}{7} \quad \frac{1}{3} \quad \frac{1}{4} \quad \frac{2}{3} \quad \frac{1}{9} \qquad \frac{5}{6} \quad \frac{7}{8} \quad \frac{1}{8} \quad \frac{2}{3} \quad \frac{3}{4} \quad \frac{7}{8} \quad \frac{5}{6}$$

Name _____ Date _____

A Giant Dinosaur

Paleontologists believe that the biggest dinosaur that ever lived measured about 120 feet (36 meters) from head to tail and was about 18 feet (5.5 meters) high. What is the name of this giant creature?

Answer:

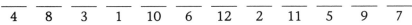

 __ __ __ __ __ __ __ __ __ __ __ __
 4   8   3   1   10 6   12 2   11 5   9   7

To answer the question, simplify each fraction and find its simplified form in the Answer Box. Then write the letter of each simplified fraction in the space above its problem number. **Hint:** Some letters will be used more than once. Others will not be used.

1 $\frac{9}{12}$ = _____	**7** $\frac{6}{8}$ = _____
2 $\frac{6}{16}$ = _____	**8** $\frac{12}{33}$ = _____
3 $\frac{8}{20}$ = _____	**9** $\frac{9}{21}$ = _____
4 $\frac{15}{20}$ = _____	**10** $\frac{15}{18}$ = _____
5 $\frac{21}{27}$ = _____	**11** $\frac{12}{28}$ = _____
6 $\frac{10}{24}$ = _____	**12** $\frac{12}{16}$ = _____

Answer Box

R. $\frac{7}{9}$

A. $\frac{3}{8}$

N. $\frac{6}{7}$

M. $\frac{5}{6}$

E. $\frac{4}{11}$

T. $\frac{7}{10}$

S. $\frac{3}{4}$

U. $\frac{3}{7}$

I. $\frac{2}{5}$

O. $\frac{5}{12}$

Giganto-Gum

Fill in words and numbers as directed.
Then solve the problem.

My _____
<small>(choose a number: 2 or 3)</small>

friends and I recently went to

_____'s Candy
<small>(last name of a famous person)</small>

Store. We usually go there to buy

comic books, _____, and candy. The store sells a new
<small>(plural noun)</small>

_____ gum called Giganto-Gum. One stick of it is
<small>(adjective)</small>

_____ inches long! It costs _____.
<small>(number greater than 10)</small>   <small>(amount of money)</small>

We pooled our money and bought one. Then we split up the gum

evenly. It tasted like _____ and smelled just like
<small>(plural noun)</small>

_____! We can't wait to get some more!
<small>(plural noun)</small>

How much Giganto-Gum
did each friend get?
Answer with a fraction. _____

Name _____ Date _____

Who wrote the book *The Beehive*?

Solve the problems.

Write each fraction in simplest form.

Solve the riddle using your answers.

	Fraction	Simplest Form
Three students picked 15 pounds of apples to share. What fraction of the 15 pounds of apples will each student take home?	___ B	___ U
Six people bought flowers. Four bought daisies. Two bought roses. What fraction bought daisies?	___ S	___ E
There are 30 students in the class. 15 are girls. What fraction are girls?	___ G	___ N
Sam walked eight dogs after school on Tuesday. Six of them were spaniels. What fraction were spaniels?	___ T	___ I

Solve the Riddle! Write the letter that goes with each answer.

___ **.**   ___ ___ ___   ___ ___ ___ ___ ___
$\frac{3}{4}$ $\frac{3}{15}$ $\frac{2}{3}$ $\frac{1}{2}$ $\frac{4}{6}$ $\frac{6}{8}$ $\frac{1}{5}$ $\frac{1}{2}$ $\frac{15}{30}$

 100 Math Practice Pages, Grade 4 © 2015 • Scholastic Teaching Resources

Name _____ Date _____

Out of Order

We're sorry, but this activity is out of order.
Solve three ordering fraction problems in a row
to get Tic-Tac-Math!

Fill in the box with
>, <, or =.

$$\frac{2}{8} \ \square \ \frac{5}{8}$$

Fill in the box with
>, <, or =.

$$\frac{2}{10} \ \square \ \frac{1}{5}$$

Fill in the box with
>, <, or =.

$$\frac{1}{2} \ \square \ \frac{1}{4}$$

Fill in the box with
>, <, or =.

$$\frac{3}{4} \ \square \ \frac{9}{12}$$

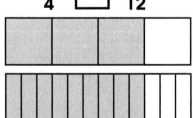

Fill in the box with
>, <, or =.

$$\frac{5}{6} \ \square \ \frac{7}{8}$$

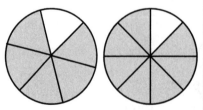

Fill in the box with
>, <, or =.

$$\frac{8}{10} \ \square \ \frac{4}{6}$$

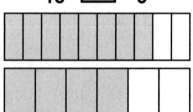

Order these fractions
from greatest to least:

$$\frac{1}{6} \qquad \frac{2}{3} \qquad \frac{1}{3}$$

____ ____ ____

Order these fractions
from greatest to least:

$$\frac{5}{8} \qquad \frac{3}{4} \qquad \frac{1}{4} \qquad \frac{3}{8}$$

____ ____ ____ ____

Order these fractions
from greatest to least:

$$\frac{3}{4} \qquad \frac{5}{6} \qquad \frac{7}{12} \qquad \frac{2}{3}$$

____ ____ ____ ____

Name _____ Date _____

Why are tennis players so noisy?

Circle the greater fraction. Solve the riddle using your answers.

$\frac{1}{2}$ or $\frac{1}{4}$	$\frac{1}{3}$ or $\frac{1}{5}$	$\frac{1}{4}$ or $\frac{1}{6}$
T B	A J	Y D
$\frac{1}{8}$ or $\frac{1}{9}$	$\frac{3}{6}$ or $\frac{4}{5}$	$\frac{1}{2}$ or $\frac{2}{3}$
H M	G K	B E
$\frac{4}{6}$ or $\frac{3}{4}$	$\frac{3}{5}$ or $\frac{3}{10}$	$\frac{5}{8}$ or $\frac{4}{16}$
W X	S U	I O
$\frac{1}{3}$ or $\frac{6}{12}$	$\frac{3}{8}$ or $\frac{1}{4}$	$\frac{1}{9}$ or $\frac{2}{6}$
N P	C F	L R

Solve the Riddle!   Write the letter that goes with each answer.

$\dfrac{1}{2}$ $\dfrac{1}{8}$ $\dfrac{2}{3}$ $\dfrac{1}{4}$ $\dfrac{2}{6}$ $\dfrac{1}{3}$ $\dfrac{5}{8}$ $\dfrac{3}{5}$ $\dfrac{2}{3}$

$\dfrac{1}{3}$ $\dfrac{2}{6}$ $\dfrac{1}{3}$ $\dfrac{3}{8}$ $\dfrac{4}{5}$ $\dfrac{2}{3}$ $\dfrac{1}{2}$.

Name _____ Date _____

Roanoke Baby

The first English child born in America was born on Roanoke Island in 1587. What was the name of this child?

Answer:

$$\frac{V}{1} \quad \frac{}{2} \quad \frac{}{3} \quad \frac{}{4} \quad \frac{}{5} \quad \frac{}{6} \quad \frac{}{7} \quad \frac{}{8} \qquad \frac{}{9} \quad \frac{}{10} \quad \frac{}{11} \quad \frac{}{12}$$

To answer the question, find the fraction that makes each comparison true. Then write the letter of each answer in the space above its problem number. The first one has been done for you.

1 $\frac{5}{8} > \underline{\frac{1}{4}}$

$\frac{10}{16}$ $\quad$ $\left(\frac{1}{4}\right)$ $\quad$ $\frac{4}{5}$

S $\qquad$ V $\qquad$ T

5 $\frac{3}{5} = \underline{\hspace{2cm}}$

$\frac{6}{9}$ $\quad$ $\frac{12}{15}$ $\quad$ $\frac{15}{25}$

H $\qquad$ U $\qquad$ I

9 $\frac{3}{4} = \underline{\hspace{2cm}}$

$\frac{10}{16}$ $\quad$ $\frac{9}{12}$ $\quad$ $\frac{12}{20}$

B $\qquad$ D $\qquad$ U

2 $\frac{7}{10} > \underline{\hspace{2cm}}$

$\frac{3}{5}$ $\quad$ $\frac{7}{8}$ $\quad$ $\frac{6}{7}$

I $\qquad$ H $\qquad$ W

6 $\frac{4}{7} < \underline{\hspace{2cm}}$

$\frac{7}{8}$ $\quad$ $\frac{1}{3}$ $\quad$ $\frac{2}{9}$

N $\qquad$ O $\qquad$ C

10 $\frac{1}{2} > \underline{\hspace{2cm}}$

$\frac{5}{7}$ $\quad$ $\frac{7}{8}$ $\quad$ $\frac{4}{11}$

M $\qquad$ Y $\qquad$ A

3 $\frac{2}{3} < \underline{\hspace{2cm}}$

$\frac{7}{12}$ $\quad$ $\frac{2}{7}$ $\quad$ $\frac{3}{4}$

O $\qquad$ T $\qquad$ R

7 $\frac{2}{5} < \underline{\hspace{2cm}}$

$\frac{3}{10}$ $\quad$ $\frac{2}{7}$ $\quad$ $\frac{5}{8}$

J $\qquad$ V $\qquad$ I

11 $\frac{6}{11} < \underline{\hspace{2cm}}$

$\frac{3}{8}$ $\quad$ $\frac{7}{10}$ $\quad$ $\frac{3}{7}$

P $\qquad$ R $\qquad$ F

4 $\frac{1}{6} > \underline{\hspace{2cm}}$

$\frac{1}{5}$ $\quad$ $\frac{1}{7}$ $\quad$ $\frac{1}{4}$

B $\qquad$ G $\qquad$ M

8 $\frac{4}{9} < \underline{\hspace{2cm}}$

$\frac{1}{3}$ $\quad$ $\frac{1}{2}$ $\quad$ $\frac{5}{13}$

K $\qquad$ A $\qquad$ T

12 $\frac{7}{12} > \underline{\hspace{2cm}}$

$\frac{5}{9}$ $\quad$ $\frac{3}{5}$ $\quad$ $\frac{5}{7}$

E $\qquad$ S $\qquad$ G

Name _____ Date _____

What did the duck wear to his wedding?

Add.

Solve the riddle using your answers.

$\dfrac{2}{4} + \dfrac{1}{4} = \underline{}$ R	$\dfrac{4}{12} + \dfrac{7}{12} = \underline{}$ A
$\dfrac{1}{5} + \dfrac{3}{5} = \underline{}$ S	$\dfrac{4}{6} + \dfrac{1}{6} = \underline{}$ D
$\dfrac{3}{8} + \dfrac{2}{8} = \underline{}$ O	$\dfrac{6}{9} + \dfrac{1}{9} = \underline{}$ L
$\dfrac{3}{7} + \dfrac{2}{7} = \underline{}$ C	$\dfrac{7}{11} + \dfrac{3}{11} = \underline{}$ N
$\dfrac{2}{8} + \dfrac{4}{8} = \underline{}$ T	$\dfrac{1}{7} + \dfrac{5}{7} = \underline{}$ K
$\dfrac{4}{10} + \dfrac{5}{10} = \underline{}$ E	$\dfrac{1}{3} + \dfrac{1}{3} = \underline{}$ U

Solve the Riddle! Write the letter that goes with each answer.

$$\underset{\frac{11}{12}}{\underline{}} \quad \underset{\frac{5}{6}}{\underline{}} \quad \underset{\frac{2}{3}}{\underline{}} \quad \underset{\frac{5}{7}}{\underline{}} \quad \underset{\frac{6}{7}}{\underline{}} \quad \underset{\frac{4}{5}}{\underline{}} \quad \overset{\textbf{—}}{\underset{\frac{9}{10}}{\underline{}}} \quad \underset{\frac{5}{6}}{\underline{}} \quad \underset{\frac{5}{8}}{\underline{}}$$

Pizza Night

**Fill in words and numbers as directed.
Then solve the problem.**

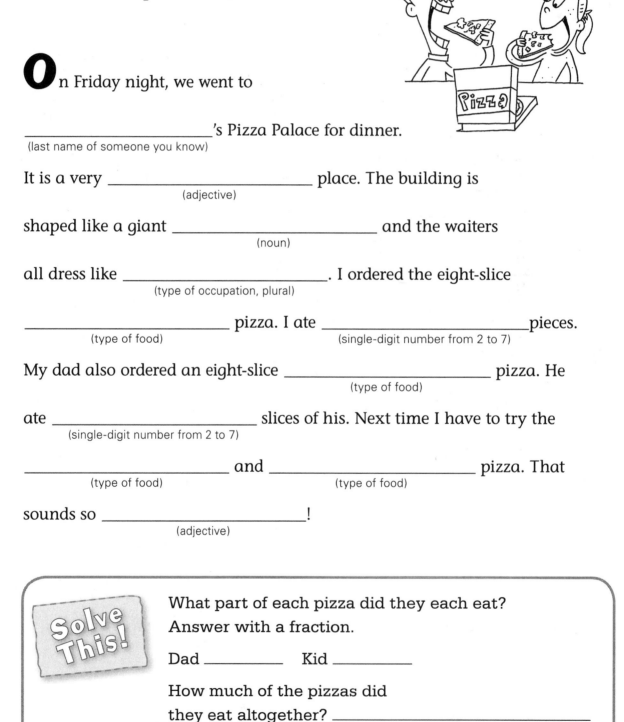

On Friday night, we went to

_____'s Pizza Palace for dinner.
(last name of someone you know)

It is a very _____ place. The building is
(adjective)

shaped like a giant _____ and the waiters
(noun)

all dress like _____. I ordered the eight-slice
(type of occupation, plural)

_____ pizza. I ate _____ pieces.
(type of food)   (single-digit number from 2 to 7)

My dad also ordered an eight-slice _____ pizza. He
(type of food)

ate _____ slices of his. Next time I have to try the
(single-digit number from 2 to 7)

_____ and _____ pizza. That
(type of food)   (type of food)

sounds so _____!
(adjective)

Solve This!

What part of each pizza did they each eat?
Answer with a fraction.

Dad _____   Kid _____

How much of the pizzas did
they eat altogether? _____

Some Fraction Sums

Find the sum or difference of each set of fractions. Be sure to simplify. Solve three problems in a row to get Tic-Tac-Math!

$$\frac{2}{4} + \frac{1}{4} =$$

$$\frac{5}{6} - \frac{2}{6} =$$

Mona got 9 out of 10 questions correct on a quiz. What fraction of the questions did she answer incorrectly?

$$\frac{3}{8} + \frac{3}{8} =$$

$$\frac{7}{10} - \frac{2}{10} =$$

Jack's new CD has 14 songs on it. He loves $\frac{5}{14}$ of its songs and really likes another $\frac{2}{14}$ of them. What fraction of the songs does Jack love or really like?

$$\frac{4}{9} + \frac{2}{9} =$$

$$\frac{10}{12} - \frac{7}{12} =$$

Lucy spent $\frac{9}{20}$ of her birthday money on sporting goods and $\frac{3}{10}$ of it on DVDs. What fraction of her birthday money did she spend in all?

A Grand Old Tree

Some of the oldest known living things on Earth are trees. One kind of tree can live for 5,000 years. What is the name of this tree?

Answer:

$$\frac{\overline{3}}{4} \quad \frac{\overline{5}}{7} \quad \frac{\overline{1}}{2} \quad 1\frac{1}{3} \quad \frac{\overline{4}}{9} \quad \frac{\overline{1}}{3} \quad \frac{\overline{2}}{3} \quad 1\frac{1}{2} \quad \frac{\overline{3}}{5} \quad \frac{\overline{5}}{6} \quad \frac{\overline{2}}{3}$$

$$1\frac{\overline{3}}{7} \quad \frac{\overline{1}}{2} \quad \frac{\overline{5}}{6} \quad \frac{\overline{2}}{3}$$

To answer the question, add or subtract each problem. Be sure your answers are simplified. Write the letter of the problem in the space above its answer. **Hint:** Some letters will be used more than once. Others will not be used.

O. $\frac{1}{5} + \frac{2}{5}$ 　　 R. $\frac{2}{7} + \frac{3}{7}$ 　　 M. $\frac{7}{8} - \frac{5}{8}$ 　　 T. $\frac{8}{9} - \frac{4}{9}$ 　　 Y. $\frac{3}{10} + \frac{7}{10}$

S. $\frac{2}{3} + \frac{2}{3}$ 　　 H. $\frac{5}{6} + \frac{5}{6}$ 　　 C. $\frac{3}{4} + \frac{3}{4}$ 　　 B. $\frac{7}{8} - \frac{1}{8}$ 　　 N. $\frac{11}{12} - \frac{1}{12}$

V. $\frac{7}{12} + \frac{7}{12}$ 　　 P. $\frac{11}{14} + \frac{9}{14}$ 　　 I. $\frac{11}{12} - \frac{5}{12}$ 　　 L. $\frac{8}{9} - \frac{5}{9}$ 　　 E. $\frac{14}{15} - \frac{4}{15}$

Name _____ Date _____

Why did Silly Billy open his toolbox in math class?

Subtract.

Solve the riddle using your answers.

$$\frac{3}{4} - \frac{1}{4} = \underline{\quad} \atop M$$

$$\frac{5}{8} - \frac{4}{8} = \underline{\quad} \atop D$$

$$\frac{5}{6} - \frac{2}{6} = \underline{\quad} \atop E$$

$$\frac{11}{12} - \frac{4}{12} = \underline{\quad} \atop R$$

$$\frac{8}{9} - \frac{3}{9} = \underline{\quad} \atop A$$

$$\frac{4}{5} - \frac{2}{5} = \underline{\quad} \atop T$$

$$\frac{6}{7} - \frac{3}{7} = \underline{\quad} \atop P$$

$$\frac{10}{11} - \frac{6}{11} = \underline{\quad} \atop N$$

$$\frac{12}{14} - \frac{4}{14} = \underline{\quad} \atop U$$

$$\frac{8}{10} - \frac{2}{10} = \underline{\quad} \atop L$$

$$\frac{13}{15} - \frac{4}{15} = \underline{\quad} \atop I$$

$$\frac{2}{3} - \frac{1}{3} = \underline{\quad} \atop H$$

Solve the Riddle! Write the letter that goes with each answer.

$$\frac{1}{3} \quad \frac{3}{6} \quad \frac{4}{11} \quad \frac{3}{6} \quad \frac{3}{6} \quad \frac{1}{8} \quad \frac{3}{6} \quad \frac{1}{8} \quad \frac{5}{9} \ .$$

$$\frac{2}{4} \quad \frac{8}{14} \quad \frac{6}{10} \quad \frac{2}{5} \quad \frac{9}{15} \quad \frac{3}{7} \quad \frac{6}{10} \quad \frac{9}{15} \quad \frac{3}{6} \quad \frac{7}{12}$$

100 Math Practice Pages, Grade 4 © 2015 • Scholastic Teaching Resources

Teeny-Tiny Plant-Growing Contest

Fill in words and numbers as directed.
Then solve the problem.

My friend _____ and I had a teeny-tiny
(first name of a boy)

plant-growing contest. I fed my plant _____. I
(plural noun)

even named it _____. My plant ended up being
(name of a famous person)

_____ tenths of an inch tall. My friend named his plant,
(single-digit number greater than 1)

too. He called it _____ _____.
(first name of a boy or girl)   (different name)

He watered his plant _____ times a day. His plant
(number greater than 1)

grew to be _____ tenths of an inch tall.
(different single-digit number greater than 1)

Both plants were _____ and beautiful. They had
(adjective)

_____ leaves and _____ stems. And
(color)   (color)

they smelled like _____!
(plural noun)

Solve This!

Which plant was tallest? _____

How much taller was it
than the other plant?
Answer with a fraction. _____

Mix-Ups in the Kitchen

Don't get mixed up by mixed numbers in the kitchen! Solve three problems in a row to get Tic-Tac-Math!

How much of the pizzas is left? Write a mixed number. _____

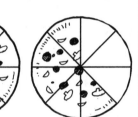

How much of the soda six-packs is left? Write a mixed number. _____

Shade the diagram to show $2\frac{3}{4}$.

Shade the diagram to show $3\frac{1}{6}$.

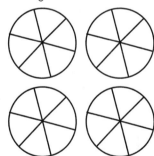

Lucille cut 2 pies into 6 slices each. If Lucille's family eats $1\frac{5}{6}$ pies, how many slices were eaten?

_____ slices

Express $\frac{8}{5}$ as a mixed number.

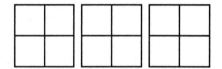

_____

Express $\frac{7}{3}$ as a mixed number.

_____

Express $2\frac{1}{2}$ as an improper fraction.

_____

Antoine is making cookies. His recipe calls for 2 cups of sugar. He has $\frac{17}{8}$ cups of sugar. Does he have enough?

yes   no

A Huge, Mysterious Life-form

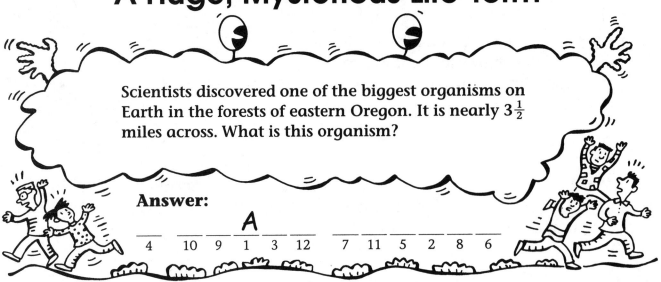

Scientists discovered one of the biggest organisms on Earth in the forests of eastern Oregon. It is nearly $3\frac{1}{2}$ miles across. What is this organism?

Answer:

$\dfrac{\ \ \ \ }{4}\ \dfrac{\ \ \ \ }{10}\ \dfrac{\ \ \ \ }{9}\ \dfrac{A}{1}\ \dfrac{\ \ \ \ }{3}\ \dfrac{\ \ \ \ }{12}\ \ \dfrac{\ \ \ \ }{7}\ \dfrac{\ \ \ \ }{11}\ \dfrac{\ \ \ \ }{5}\ \dfrac{\ \ \ \ }{2}\ \dfrac{\ \ \ \ }{8}\ \dfrac{\ \ \ \ }{6}$

To answer the question above, convert each improper fraction to a mixed number in the simplest form. Find each answer in the Answer Box. Then write the corresponding letter in the space above its problem number. The first one has been done for you.
Hint: Not all letters will be used.

Answer Box
U. $1\frac{7}{12}$
T. $2\frac{1}{5}$
F. $2\frac{1}{3}$
D. $2\frac{2}{5}$
A. $2\frac{2}{3}$
B. $3\frac{1}{5}$
R. $3\frac{1}{3}$
N. $3\frac{3}{7}$
I. $4\frac{1}{4}$
A. $4\frac{2}{3}$
N. $5\frac{1}{3}$
G. $5\frac{2}{5}$
U. $5\frac{1}{2}$
S. $9\frac{1}{3}$
G. $9\frac{1}{2}$

1 $\dfrac{8}{3} = \underline{\ 2\frac{2}{3}\ }$

2 $\dfrac{27}{5} = \underline{\ \ \ \ \ }$

3 $\dfrac{24}{7} = \underline{\ \ \ \ \ }$

4 $\dfrac{14}{3} = \underline{\ \ \ \ \ }$

5 $\dfrac{32}{6} = \underline{\ \ \ \ \ }$

6 $\dfrac{56}{6} = \underline{\ \ \ \ \ }$

7 $\dfrac{21}{9} = \underline{\ \ \ \ \ }$

8 $\dfrac{44}{8} = \underline{\ \ \ \ \ }$

9 $\dfrac{17}{4} = \underline{\ \ \ \ \ }$

10 $\dfrac{38}{4} = \underline{\ \ \ \ \ }$

11 $\dfrac{19}{12} = \underline{\ \ \ \ \ }$

12 $\dfrac{22}{10} = \underline{\ \ \ \ \ }$

What do you use to fix an orangutan robot?

Rename the improper fractions as mixed or whole numbers. Solve the riddle using your answers.

$$\frac{50}{5} = \underline{} \atop E$$

$$\frac{5}{3} = \underline{} \atop H$$

$$\frac{11}{6} = \underline{} \atop K$$

$$\frac{7}{7} = \underline{} \atop Y$$

$$\frac{32}{4} = \underline{} \atop C$$

$$\frac{15}{4} = \underline{} \atop M$$

$$\frac{17}{2} = \underline{} \atop W$$

$$\frac{21}{7} = \underline{} \atop R$$

$$\frac{17}{7} = \underline{} \atop T$$

$$\frac{11}{3} = \underline{} \atop N$$

$$\frac{18}{3} = \underline{} \atop A$$

$$\frac{15}{8} = \underline{} \atop O$$

Solve the Riddle! Write the letter that goes with each answer.

$$\overline{6} \quad \overline{3\frac{3}{4}} \quad \overline{1\frac{7}{8}} \quad \overline{3\frac{2}{3}} \quad \overline{1\frac{5}{6}} \quad \overline{10} \quad \overline{1}$$

$$\overline{8\frac{1}{2}} \quad \overline{3} \quad \overline{10} \quad \overline{3\frac{2}{3}} \quad \overline{8} \quad \overline{1\frac{2}{3}}$$

The Western Hemisphere

Christopher Columbus reached North America in 1492. But another man led a group of Europeans to the coast of North America nearly 500 years earlier. Who was this man?

Answer:

$\overline{2\frac{5}{7}}$ $\overline{7\frac{3}{5}}$ $\overline{4\frac{2}{3}}$ $\overline{4\frac{1}{3}}$ $\quad$ $\overline{7\frac{3}{5}}$ $\overline{2\frac{2}{3}}$ $\overline{4\frac{2}{3}}$ $\overline{1\frac{2}{7}}$ $\overline{3\frac{1}{4}}$ $\overline{3\frac{1}{4}}$ $\overline{6\frac{3}{5}}$ $\overline{6}$

To answer the question, add or subtract the mixed numbers. Be sure your answers are simplified. Write the letter of the problem in the space above its answer. **Hint:** Some letters will be used more than once. Others will not be used.

C. $\quad 4\frac{3}{7}$
$\quad -\ 3\frac{1}{7}$

R. $\quad 4\frac{7}{8}$
$\quad -\ 2\frac{1}{8}$

S. $\quad 8\frac{13}{16}$
$\quad -\ 5\frac{9}{16}$

W. $\quad 5\frac{6}{7}$
$\quad -\ 2\frac{3}{7}$

M. $\quad 4\frac{3}{8}$
$\quad +\ 2\frac{1}{8}$

E. $\quad 12\frac{9}{10}$
$\quad -\ 5\frac{3}{10}$

O. $\quad 3\frac{2}{5}$
$\quad +\ 3\frac{1}{5}$

N. $\quad 3\frac{1}{3}$
$\quad +\ 2\frac{2}{3}$

H. $\quad 6\frac{7}{12}$
$\quad +\ 4\frac{7}{12}$

J. $\quad 5\frac{5}{6}$
$\quad -\ 3$

F. $\quad 7\frac{5}{9}$
$\quad -\ 3\frac{2}{9}$

L. $\quad 9\frac{11}{14}$
$\quad -\ 7\frac{1}{14}$

I. $\quad 3\frac{3}{3}$
$\quad +\ 1\frac{1}{3}$

A. $\quad 3\frac{3}{4}$
$\quad +\ 3\frac{1}{4}$

D. $\quad 5\frac{3}{8}$
$\quad +\ 4\frac{1}{8}$

Name _____ Date _____

Fractions in Action!

Be a fraction hero: Solve three fraction problems in a row to get Tic-Tac-Math!

Shade $\frac{1}{4}$ of the 20 counters.

○ ○ ○ ○ ○
○ ○ ○ ○ ○
○ ○ ○ ○ ○
○ ○ ○ ○ ○

Shade $\frac{2}{3}$ of the 18 counters.

○ ○ ○ ○ ○ ○
○ ○ ○ ○ ○ ○
○ ○ ○ ○ ○ ○

Shade $\frac{5}{7}$ of the 28 counters.

○ ○ ○ ○ ○ ○ ○
○ ○ ○ ○ ○ ○ ○
○ ○ ○ ○ ○ ○ ○
○ ○ ○ ○ ○ ○ ○

What is $\frac{1}{2}$ of 30? _____

What is $\frac{3}{5}$ of 15? _____

What is $\frac{5}{8}$ of 32? _____

Julie had 24 chocolate candies. She gave $\frac{1}{4}$ of them to her brother Gary. How many candies did she give to Gary?

_____ candies

Andrew saw his grandmother on $\frac{2}{7}$ of the days in the past two weeks. (Two weeks is 14 days.) How many days did Andrew see his grandmother?

_____ days

Rachel and Gregory played 36 games of chess. Rachel won $\frac{5}{9}$ of the games. How many games did Rachel win?

_____ games

Name _____ Date _____

What happened to the bike made of wood?

Multiply. Write the answers in simplest form.

Solve the riddle using your answers.

$3 \times \dfrac{4}{6} =$ _____ S

$5 \times \dfrac{4}{7} =$ _____ A

$2 \times \dfrac{2}{12} =$ _____ T

$4 \times \dfrac{3}{8} =$ _____ R

$8 \times \dfrac{3}{7} =$ _____ O

$2 \times \dfrac{3}{10} =$ _____ N

$7 \times \dfrac{2}{3} =$ _____ W

$5 \times \dfrac{6}{9} =$ _____ I

$3 \times \dfrac{3}{4} =$ _____ G

$7 \times \dfrac{1}{5} =$ _____ D

$8 \times \dfrac{3}{2} =$ _____ E

$8 \times \dfrac{7}{9} =$ _____ L

Solve the Riddle! Write the letter that goes with each answer.

$\overline{\quad}$ $\overline{\quad}$ $\overline{\quad}$ $\overline{\quad}$ $\overline{\quad}$ $\overline{\quad}$ $\overline{\quad}$ $\overline{\quad}$ $\overline{\quad}$ $\overline{\quad}$.
$3\frac{1}{3}$ $\frac{1}{3}$ $4\frac{2}{3}$ $3\frac{3}{7}$ $3\frac{3}{7}$ $1\frac{2}{5}$ 12 $\frac{3}{5}$ $2\frac{1}{4}$ $3\frac{3}{7}$

Road Race

Fill in words and numbers as directed.
Then solve the problem.

The _____ Annual
(ordinal number)

_____ Road Race
(name of a place)

will take place this weekend. You have to run around the town of

_____ _____ times. Each lap
(name of a town) (single-digit number greater than 1)

around is _____ mile. You run as part of a team.
(choose a number: $\frac{1}{4}$, $\frac{1}{3}$, or any other fraction)

My team is the _____ _____ .
(adjective) (plural noun)

The hard part is you have to carry two _____ and
(plural noun)

pass them to a team member at the end of your lap. You also have to

wear _____ because the weather will most likely be
(type of clothing)

_____ . I am up for the challenge, though. I know
(adjective)

I will _____ _____ !
(present-tense verb) (adverb ending in –ly)

How many miles long
is the Road Race? _____

What do you call matches that won't light up?

For each underlined number, circle the correct place value. Solve the riddle using your answers.

7.9<u>5</u>	3.5<u>0</u>	<u>4</u>.31
N 5 hundredths	I 0 hundredths	I 4 hundredths
C 5 tenths	K 0 tenths	W 4 tenths
H 5 ones	M 0 ones	Y 4 ones

6.<u>1</u>2	<u>6</u>.84	1.2<u>9</u>
V 1 hundredth	D 6 hundredths	T 9 hundredths
R 1 tenth	I 6 tenths	B 9 tenths
N 1 one	O 6 ones	R 9 ones

<u>2</u>.46	9.<u>7</u>3	5.<u>8</u>7
G 2 hundredths	R 7 hundredths	P 8 hundredths
Q 2 tenths	E 7 tenths	K 8 tenths
S 2 ones	Z 7 ones	D 8 ones

Solve the Riddle!   Write the letter that goes with each answer.

__	__	__	__	__	__	__	__
6 ones	5 hundredths	2 ones	9 hundredths	1 tenth	0 hundredths	8 tenths	7 tenths

Name _____   Date _____

Decimal I.D.

Write the decimal for each part.

1

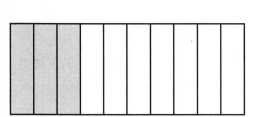

_____

2

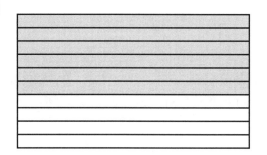

_____

3

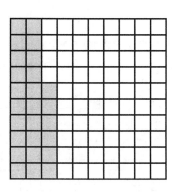

_____

4

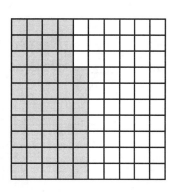

_____

5

Write each decimal in number form.

three tenths _____   seven hundredths _____

sixty-two hundredths _____   sixteen hundredths _____

nine tenths _____   one hundredth _____

Crazy About Decimals!

You may not love decimals as much as this kid does! You'll get to like them when you solve three problems in a row and get Tic-Tac-Math!

Name the shaded part as a decimal: _____

Name the shaded part as a decimal: _____

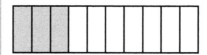

Name the shaded part as a decimal: _____

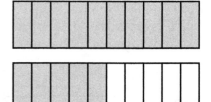

Name the shaded part as a decimal: _____

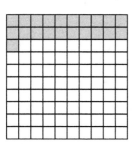

Name the shaded part as a decimal: _____

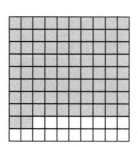

Name the shaded part as a decimal: _____

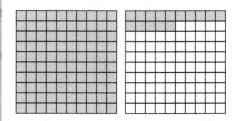

Order these decimals from least to greatest:

____ 5.65
____ 5.56
____ 5.6
____ 5.5

Order these decimals from least to greatest:

____ 10.34
____ 10.43
____ 10.04
____ 10.4
____ 10.3
____ 10.14

Order these decimals from least to greatest:

____ 4.85
____ 4.58
____ 4.9
____ 4.8
____ 4.81
____ 4.5

Classroom Fix-Up

**Fill in words and numbers as directed.
Then solve the problem.**

Our teacher, _____,
(name of a famous person)

decided it was time to fix up our classroom.

We all shared in the work. We started by

cleaning out all the old _____. Then we scrubbed
(plural noun)

the floor with _____. We straightened our
(type of substance)

desks and _____ them. The room was looking
(verb ending in -ed)

_____, but we weren't finished yet. We divided one wall
(adjective)

into ten sections. We bought _____ paint and started
(color)

painting. We got _____ sections of the wall painted.
(single-digit number greater than 1)

It's going a little slowly because we have been _____
(verb ending in -ing)

at the same time, but we'll be finished soon. Our teacher says it should only

take another _____ days.
(number greater than 1)

How much of the wall was painted?
Answer with a decimal. _____

Decimal Mix-Up

These decimals are all mixed up.
Follow the directions to put
them back in order.

Order the decimals from least to greatest.

1.   1.6   1.2   1.9   1.5   _____

2.   6.4   6.7   6.8   6.1   _____

3.   1.06   1.02   1.92   1.05   _____

4.   6.43   6.73   4.47   6.14   _____

Order the decimals from greatest to least.

5. 10.1   10.9   0.4   10.6   _____

6. 12.7   12.3   11.9   12.8   _____

7. 10.01   10.91   9.99   10.06   _____

8. 12.37   11.23   10.16   12.23   _____

Name _____ Date _____

A Special Kind of Scientist

Scientists who study birds are called ornithologists. Scientists who study insects are known as entomologists. What are scientists who study reptiles called?

Answer:

—————————————————————————————————————
6   9   3   12   1   10   5   8   4   14   2   11   13   7

To answer the question, match each decimal with its equivalent fraction in the Answer Box. Write the letter of the fraction in the space above the problem number. **Hint:** Fractions are in simplest form.

1   0.3 = _____

2   1.29 = _____

3   0.2 = _____

4   6.7 = _____

5   0.09 = _____

6   5.75 = _____

7   0.50 = _____

8   4.7 = _____

9   0.59 = _____

10   5.45 = _____

11   0.05 = _____

12   0.88 = _____

13   0.03 = _____

14   0.22 = _____

Answer Box

O. $\frac{9}{100}$	R. $\frac{1}{5}$
L. $4\frac{7}{10}$	S. $\frac{1}{2}$
T. $\frac{3}{100}$	I. $1\frac{29}{100}$
P. $\frac{22}{25}$	G. $\frac{11}{50}$
E. $\frac{3}{10}$	T. $5\frac{9}{20}$
H. $5\frac{3}{4}$	O. $6\frac{7}{10}$
E. $\frac{59}{100}$	S. $\frac{1}{20}$

Name _____ Date _____

What do you call a funny chicken?

Write each fraction as a decimal.

Solve the riddle using your answers.

$$\frac{34}{100} = \underline{\quad}_{I}$$

$$\frac{1}{10} = \underline{\quad}_{F}$$

$$\frac{2}{10} = \underline{\quad}_{C}$$

$$\frac{17}{100} = \underline{\quad}_{A}$$

$$\frac{61}{100} = \underline{\quad}_{E}$$

$$\frac{4}{10} = \underline{\quad}_{O}$$

$$\frac{5}{10} = \underline{\quad}_{H}$$

$$\frac{1}{100} = \underline{\quad}_{M}$$

$$\frac{8}{10} = \underline{\quad}_{D}$$

$$\frac{99}{100} = \underline{\quad}_{G}$$

$$\frac{5}{100} = \underline{\quad}_{K}$$

$$\frac{74}{100} = \underline{\quad}_{N}$$

Solve the Riddle! Write the letter that goes with each answer.

$$\underline{\quad}\ \underline{\quad}\ \underline{\quad}\ \underline{\quad}\ \underline{\quad}\ \underline{\quad}\ \underline{\quad}\ \overset{\textbf{—}}{}\ \underline{\quad}\ \underline{\quad}\ \underline{\quad}$$

.17   .2   .4   .01   .61   .8   .34   .5   .61   .74

Name _____ Date _____

Fast Math

Complete each set of problems below.

1. Write a decimal equal to each fraction or mixed number.

$\frac{2}{5}$ _____ $\frac{2}{8}$ _____ $1\frac{1}{2}$ _____

$3\frac{9}{10}$ _____ $2\frac{6}{8}$ _____ $1\frac{3}{4}$ _____

$7\frac{1}{4}$ _____ $\frac{7}{10}$ _____ $5\frac{5}{5}$ _____

$\frac{6}{25}$ _____ $11\frac{3}{100}$ _____ $20\frac{15}{100}$ _____

2. Write a fraction or mixed number equal to each decimal.

0.35 _____   4.6 _____   3.75 _____

0.17 _____   5.97 _____   4.63 _____

0.85 _____   60.5 _____   99.99 _____

2.02 _____   0.07 _____   75.75 _____

Name _____ Date _____

Why did everyone want Cake on their team?

Circle the greater number.
Solve the riddle using your answers.

3.0 or .30	8.1 or 8.01
S M	T Y
4.06 or 4.60	5.55 or 5.5
F J	G Q
1.05 or 1.5	21.21 or 21.211
L H	C B
7.11 or 7.011	6.0 or 6.1
A U	F W
11.8 or 1.18	7.65 or 7.56
D I	E N
9.177 or 9.7	2.067 or 2.6
X R	V O

Solve the Riddle! Write the letter that goes with each answer.

__ __ __ __ __ __ __ __ __ __ __
3.0 1.5 7.65 6.1 7.11 3.0 7.11 5.55 2.6 2.6 11.8

__ __ __ __ __ __ .
21.211 7.11 8.1 8.1 7.65 9.7

Name _____ Date _____

Contest at the Fair

Fill in words and numbers as directed.
Then solve the problem.

I went to the _____ County
(ordinal number)

Fair yesterday. There are rides there like the Haunted

_____ and the Tunnel of _____.
(noun)   (plural noun)

There's lots of delicious food, too, like Cotton _____
(plural noun)

and Hot _____. But I was there to enter my
(plural noun)

_____ in the Biggest Vegetable Contest. People call me
(type of vegetable)

the Master Gardener, and the vegetable I entered shows why. It weighed

_____ ounces! My arch rival, _____,
(decimal number greater than 1)   (first name of a girl)

entered one that weighed _____ ounces. After the
(different decimal number greater than 1)

contest, though, we shook hands and shared a _____.
(type of beverage)

We even rode on the Spinning _____ together.
(plural noun)

Whose vegetable weighed more? _____

By how much? _____
Answer with a decimal.

Name _____ Date _____

Fraction and Decimal Party

Complete each set of problems below.

1. Finish labeling the number line to show equivalent decimals and fractions.

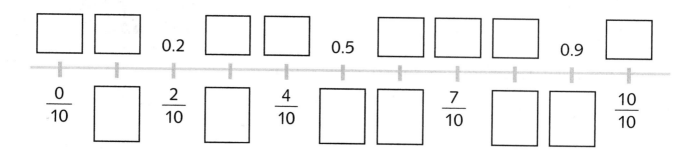

| ☐ | ☐ | 0.2 | ☐ | ☐ | 0.5 | ☐ | ☐ | ☐ | 0.9 | ☐ |

$\frac{0}{10}$ ☐ $\frac{2}{10}$ ☐ $\frac{4}{10}$ ☐ ☐ $\frac{7}{10}$ ☐ ☐ $\frac{10}{10}$

2. Write 3 decimals that belong between the given numbers.

2 < _____ < 3   9 > _____ > 8

12 < _____ < 13   80 > _____ > 79

5.5 < _____ < 6   3.2 > _____ > 3.1

3. Write the decimal from the balloon that each clue. One number is *not* used.

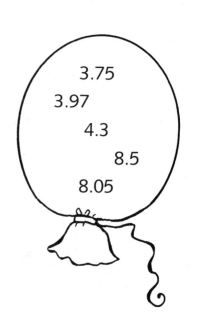

3.75
3.97
4.3
8.5
8.05

_____ is much nearer to 8 than to 9.

_____ is halfway between 8 and 9.

_____ is the same as three and three fourths.

_____ is a little less than 4.

Name _____   Date _____

Estimate It!

Read each question. Think carefully.
Then circle the best estimate.

1 About how long is your arm?

     1 foot   1 yard

2 About what is the distance between home and school?

     5 miles   500 miles

3 About how heavy is a cat?

     10 pounds   50 pounds

4 About how long is a crayon?

     15 inches   5 inches

5 About how heavy is a book?

     2 pounds   30 pounds

6 About how wide is your hand?

     7 centimeters   7 meters

7 About how much milk do you drink during a meal?

     1 gallon   1 cup

8 About how wide is your classroom door?

     3 yards   3 feet

9 About what temperature is best for a swim in an outdoor pool?

     90°F   35°F

10 About what temperature is cold enough for a heavy coat?

     28°F   75°F

A Math Laugh

Draw a circle around the answer to each of these questions to find the answer to a silly riddle.

Length

1. Which of these is the most likely measurement for the height of a door?

    C. 3 feet   **D.** 50 feet   **E.** 7 feet

2. Which of these should be used to measure the height of a building?

    A. feet   **B.** inches   **C.** miles

3. Which of these is the most likely height of a giraffe?

    H. 15 inches   **I.** 15 feet   **J.** 15 yards

Capacity

4. Which of these should be used to measure the amount of water in a swimming pool?

    B. quarts   **C.** gallons   **D.** ounces

5. Which of these is the smallest unit of measurement

    C. gallon   **D.** pint   **E.** quart

6. Which of these is the most likely amount in a glass of milk?

    P. 25 cups   **Q.** 1 quart   **R.** 8 ounces

Weight

7. Which of these has a weight that should be measured in pounds?

    S. a feather   **T.** a human baby   **u.** a grape

8. Which of these is the most likely weight of an elephant?

    Q. 4 pounds   **R.** 4 tons   **S.** 4 ounces

Write the letters of the answers you chose on the lines above the numbers for the questions.

How do you charge a battery?

With a $\underline{C}$ $\underline{}$ $\underline{}$ $\underline{}$ $\underline{}$ $\underline{}$ $\underline{}$ $\underline{D}$

        6   1   5   3   7   4   2   8

Name _____ Date _____

Amazing Feet and Inches

It shouldn't take you "long" to get Tic-Tac-Math!
Just solve three measurement problems in a row.

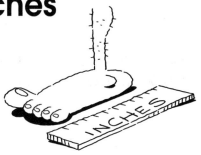

4 feet = _____ inches	5 feet = _____ inches	3 feet, 2 inches = _____ inches
2 yards = _____ feet	4 yards, 2 feet = _____ feet	1 mile = _____ feet
2 miles = _____ yards	1 mile, 300 feet = _____ feet	Frank ran 2,100 yards from school to home in 7 minutes. How would you express that distance in miles and feet? _____

Name _____ Date _____

Math Workouts

Solve each word problem.
Show your work in the tank.

1. A golfer hit a 250-yard
   shot and then a 130-yard
   shot to the hole. How
   many feet did she
   hit the ball, in total?

   _____

2. Jasmine ran 4 kilometers
   at the local track. If each
   lap is 400 meters, how
   many times did she run
   around the track?

   _____

Time for School!

Anita is keeping track of time during a school day. Take a few minutes to solve three problems in a row and get Tic-Tac-Math!

Anita wakes up at 6:00 A.M. She lays in bed for another 15 minutes. At what time does she get up?	Anita eats breakfast from 7:00 A.M. until 7:22 A.M. For how long does she eat breakfast?	One day, Anita missed the bus and got to school at 8:18 A.M. But school started at 8:00 A.M.! How late was Anita?
Anita's first class starts at 8:00 A.M. It is a double-math class that lasts 1 hour and 35 minutes. At what time does math class end?	Anita's gym class runs from 10:30 A.M. until 11:15 A.M. How long is gym class?	Anita's whole school day lasts from 8:00 A.M. to 2:30 P.M. How long is that?
Yesterday afternoon, Anita played soccer after school from 2:45 P.M. until 4:12 P.M. For how long did she play?	One day, a school assembly ran from 9:40 A.M. until 12:05 P.M. How long was the assembly?	After a busy school day, Anita was so tired, she slept from 6:52 P.M. until 6:40 A.M. For how long did Anita sleep?

Name _____ Date _____

Time for Math

What time is it? It's time to solve some math problems! Remember to read each problem carefully.

1

Ari left the airport at 11:45 A.M. He drove for 55 minutes to get home. What time did he arrive?

2

The first modern Olympics was held in 1896. The winning time in the 100-meter dash was 12 seconds. In 2008 the winning time was 9.69 seconds. How much faster was the 2008 winning time?

3

How many seconds are there in a day?

4

Krin danced for 30 minutes every morning and for 45 minutes every afternoon for 5 days. How many hours and minutes did he dance in all?

Thirst for Math

Solve each word problem.
Show your work in the tank.

1. Jada bought a 64-ounce container of apple juice. How many full 6-ounce glasses of juice can she serve her friends?

_____

2. A punch recipe calls for 3 quarts of cranberry juice, 1 quart of orange juice, and 1 gallon of club soda. How many cups of cranberry juice does the recipe need?

_____

Name _____ Date _____

Working With Weight

Solve the problems below. Remember to read each problem carefully.

1. The average mass of a cat's brain is 3.3 grams. That is 0.8 grams more than the average rabbit brain. What is the mass of the average rabbit brain?

   _____

2. Francesca bought 20 pounds of grapes for the big party. If she put 0.5 pounds in each bag, how many bags of grapes did she have?

   _____

3. Six community gardens shared equally a 225-pound bag of seeds. How many pounds does each garden get?

   _____

4. A pound equals about 2.2 kilograms. A baby elephant can weigh up to 120 kilograms. About how many pounds is that?

   _____

Supermarket Math

Mia is trying to decide what to buy. Use the information from the sales flyer to answer the questions.

This Week's Specials!

Bananas	$ 0.79 per pound
Apples	$ 0.59 per pound
Peanuts	$ 0.99 per pound
Grapes	$ 2.49 per pound
Fish	$7.60 per pound
Steak	$9.50 per pound

1
What is the cost of 3 pounds of grapes and 2 pounds of apples?

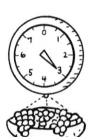

2
What is the cost of 4 pounds of bananas and 7 pounds of grapes?

3
What is the cost of 4 pounds of fish and 10 pounds of peanuts?

4
What is the cost of 2 pounds of steak and 3 pounds of fish?

5
What is the cost of 2 pounds of peanuts and 5 pounds of steak?

6
What is the cost of 5 pounds of apples and 5 pounds of fish?

Multi-Step Menu

Welcome to Benny's Burger Palace. Use the prices on the menu board to add up each customer's total. Solve three problems in a row to get Tic-Tac-Math!

Benny Burger Palace Menu

BIG Big Burger	$2.99
Baby Burger	$2.00
Chick Chick Sandwich	$2.50
Small Fries	$1.00
Super-Duper Fries	$3.00
Tiny Soda	$.50
Mega Soda	$2.49

A customer orders 4 Baby Burgers. What is his total?	A customer orders 2 Chick Chick Sandwiches. What is her total?	A customer orders 2 Super-Duper Fries and 1 Tiny Soda. What is his total?
A customer orders 2 Big Big Burgers. What is her total?	A customer orders 1 Chick Chick Sandwich and 2 Mega Sodas. What is his total?	A customer orders 2 Baby Burgers and 2 Tiny Sodas. What is her total?
A customer orders 2 Big Big Burgers, 2 Baby Burgers, 1 Super-Duper Fries, and 1 Mega Soda. What is his total?	A customer orders 3 Baby Burgers, 2 Super-Duper Fries, and 3 Mega Sodas. What is her total?	A customer orders 4 Big Big Burgers, 3 Super-Duper Fries, and 4 Mega Sodas. What is his total?

Lights Out!

One day, there was an electrical power outage at a local store where Alvaro works part-time as a checkout cashier. He had to find the total cost of items and make change without the use of the cash register or even a calculator! Solve the following problems just like Alvaro had to.

1. One customer bought a package of 12 rolls of paper towels for $5.99 and a hairbrush for $6.99. What was the total cost of these purchases? _____

   The customer paid with a $20 bill. How much change should she receive? _____

   What is the least amount of bills and coins Alvaro should use to make the proper change? _____

2. One customer bought a small hand shovel for $8.99, three bags of potting soil for $1.59 each, and two flowerpots for $4.69 each. What was the total cost of these purchases? _____

   The customer paid with a $50 bill. How much change should he receive? _____

   What is the least amount of bills and coins Alvaro should use to make the proper change? _____

3. One customer bought a set of batteries for $3.99, a box of envelopes for $3.79, a package of loose-leaf paper for $3.69, and a calculator for $9.95. What was the total cost of these purchases? _____

   She paid with a $20 bill and a $10 bill. How much change should she receive? _____

   What is the least amount of bills and coins Alvaro should use to make the proper change? _____

Name _____ Date _____

Real-Life Math

Solve the area and perimeter problems below.

AREA

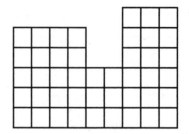

1. Find the area of the figure.

   Area = _____ square units

2. A tennis court is a rectangle 78 feet long
   and 27 feet wide. What is the area of a
   tennis court?

   Area = _____ square feet

PERIMETER

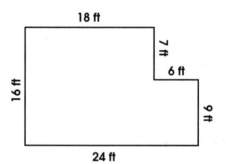

3. What is the perimeter of
   Tran's apartment?

   Perimeter = _____ feet

4. Kim's backyard is 9 meters wide. It is
   twice as long as it is wide. What is the
   perimeter of the yard?

   Perimeter = _____ meters

Lucy the Landscaper

Lucy helps her father with his landscaping business whenever she can. She understands measurement, which is an important skill for the work she does. Answer the following questions. Use the following formulas: $P = s + s + s + s$ and $A = l \ x \ w$.

1 When Lucy's father got a job to enclose a yard with a fence, he asked her to help him find how much fencing they would need. The area to be fenced was a rectangle, 102 feet by 96 feet. Her father told Lucy that the gate for the driveway would be 12 feet wide and should not be included with the total amount of fencing needed. How many feet of fencing would they need to enclose the yard?

_____

The fence the customer wanted came in sections of 8 feet. How many sections have to be ordered?

_____

Each section costs $15.99. How much will the fence cost?

_____

2 The next job involved reseeding a customer's lawn. Only the backyard and front yard needed reseeding. The dimensions of the backyard were 98 feet by 64 feet. What was the area of the backyard?

_____

A patio with dimensions of 16 feet by 14 feet was also in the backyard. What was the area of the patio?

_____

Since grass seed was not needed for the area covered by the patio, what was the area of the backyard that had to be reseeded?

_____

The dimensions of the front lawn were 42 feet by 48 feet. What was the area of the front lawn?

_____

What was the total area of the yard that had to be reseeded?

_____

3 One of their customers asked Lucy and her dad to make a rectangular flowerbed 16 feet long by 12 feet wide. What was the area of the flowerbed?

_____

To provide good coverage, 3 flowers should be planted for every square foot. How many flowers should be planted in the flowerbed?

_____

The customer would also like plastic edging to be placed around the flowerbed. Assuming the edging is placed on each side, how much edging is needed?

_____

Name _____ Date _____

Ready to Read

The line plot shows the number of hours students said they spent reading each week.

Use the data in the line plot to answer the questions.

Hours Students Spent Reading

```
                        X
                        X
    X                   X
    X    X    X    X
    X    X    X    X
    X    X    X    X    X
    X    X    X    X    X    X
    X    X    X    X    X    X                   X
  _____
    1    2    3    4    5    6    7    8    9    10
```

1. How many students were surveyed? _____

2. What is the range of the data? _____

3. What is the mode of the data? _____

4. How many students say they read for 5 hours each

   week? _____

5. An outlier is a value that "lies outside" (or away from)

   the rest of the data. Which number of hours is an outlier? _____

Name _____   Date _____

Totally Snowy!

How much snow did the town of Blizzardville get this past winter? Read this line graph to find out. You should have "snow" problem solving three problems in a row to get Tic-Tac-Math!

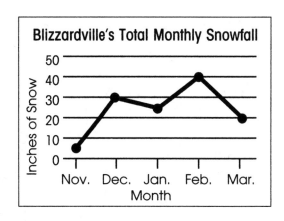

Blizzardville's Total Monthly Snowfall

In which month was there the greatest amount of snowfall?	Did the total snowfall increase or decrease between December and January?	How many inches of snow fell in March?
How many inches of snow fell in February?	How many inches of snow fell in November?	Do you think the amount of snowfall increased, decreased, or stayed the same between March and April?
How much less snow was there in November than there was in March?	In which month was there about twice as much snow as there was in March?	In which month was there about 10 inches less snowfall than there was in December?

    100 Math Practice Pages, Grade 4 © 2015 • Scholastic Teaching Resources

Surf's Up!

Kristen's parents own a surf shop. One day while Kristen was helping in the shop, her mother and father were tallying the number of surfboards they sold during the year. Kristen suggested that they use a line graph to represent the data. Study the line graph, then solve the problems.

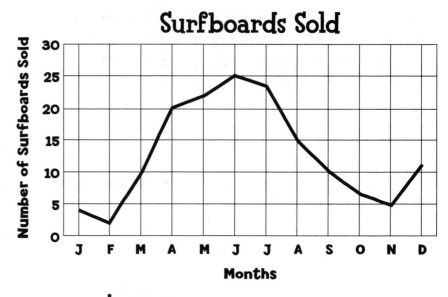

1 In which month were the greatest number of surfboards sold?

_____

How many were sold this month?

_____

2 In which month were the least number of surfboards sold?

_____

How many were sold this month?

_____

3 In which three successive months did the sale of surfboards increase the most?

_____

4 In which three successive months did the sale of surfboards decrease the most?

_____

5 How many surfboards were sold in May?   _____

How many surfboards were sold in August?   _____

How many surfboards were sold in October?   _____

6 According to the graph, what are the two best months for selling surfboards?

_____

7 During which season are the fewest surfboards sold?

_____

8 Describe the pattern of surfboard sales. What might be the reasons for this pattern?

_____

_____

Norton's Novelties

Norton's Novelty Shop sells tricks that make people laugh and scream. Norton has made a graph to show this weekend's sales for five of his popular novelties. Use his bar graph to answer the questions below.

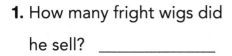

1. How many fright wigs did

   he sell? _____

2. Which of his novelties sold

   the best that weekend?

   _____

3. Which of his novelties had the fewest

   sales that weekend? _____

4. How many fright wigs and wind-up mice did

   he sell in all? _____

5. Which had more sales: fake fangs or

   rubber snakes? _____

6. How many more rubber snakes than squirting

   pens did he sell? _____

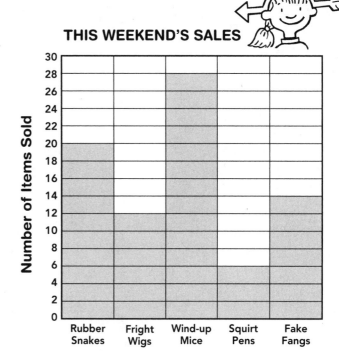

THIS WEEKEND'S SALES

Number of Items Sold — values: 0, 2, 4, 6, 8, 10, 12, 14, 16, 18, 20, 22, 24, 26, 28, 30

Categories: Rubber Snakes, Fright Wigs, Wind-up Mice, Squirt Pens, Fake Fangs

Popular Novelties

Bonus! How many sales in all does his bar graph show? _____

All Kinds of Lines

You're not just getting a line here. Solve three problems in a row to get Tic-Tac-Math! Write your answer below the figure.

Is this a line, a ray, or a line segment?

Is this a line, a ray, or a line segment?

Is this a line, a ray, or a line segment?

Are the lines intersecting or parallel?

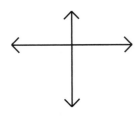

Are the lines intersecting or parallel?

Are the lines intersecting or parallel?

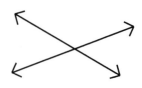

Are the lines parallel or perpendicular?

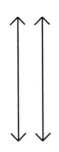

Are the lines parallel or perpendicular?

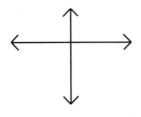

Are the lines parallel or perpendicular?

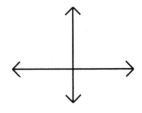

What's My Angle?

Study the angles and polygons below.
Then answer the questions.

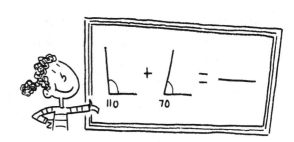

1 Is this angle greater than, less than, or equal to a right angle? _____ 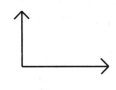	**2** Is this angle greater than, less than, or equal to a right angle? _____ 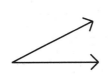	**3** Is this angle greater than, less than, or equal to a right angle? _____ 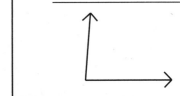
4 Is this an acute, obtuse, or right angle? _____ 	**5** Is this an acute, obtuse, or right angle? _____ 	**6** Is this an acute, obtuse, or right angle? _____ 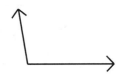
7 Is this triangle acute, obtuse, or right? _____ 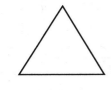	**8** Is this triangle acute, obtuse, or right? _____ 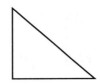	**9** Is this triangle acute, obtuse, or right? _____ 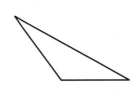

100 Math Practice Pages, Grade 4 © 2015 • Scholastic Teaching Resources

Name _____   Date _____

Symmetrical Designs

Half of each design appears above a line of symmetry.
Shade the rest of the design. Keep it symmetrical.

1.
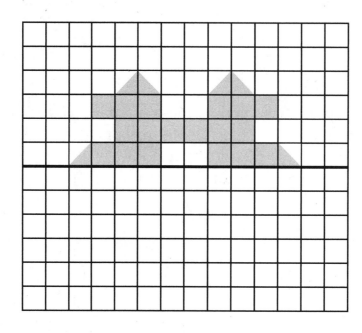

2.
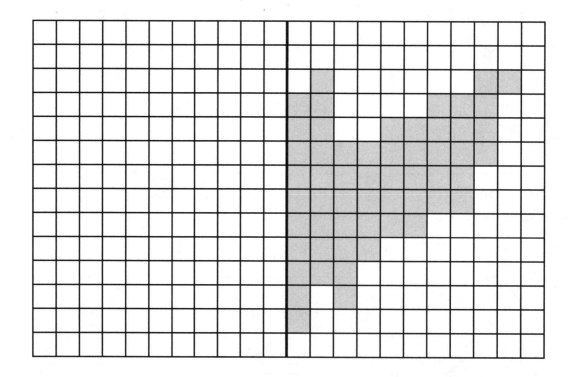

Practice Page 1:

<	>	<
=	>	<

4,582	30,458	560,987
5,725	31,008	567,089
5,820	31,201	567,098
5,872	32,000	567,890
	38,562	567,980

Practice Page 2:

1. <	7. <
2. >	8. >
3. <	9. <
4. <	10. =
5. <	11. <
6. >	12. >

Practice Page 3:

Practice Page 4:

1. tens
2. hundreds
3. ten thousands
4. thousands
5. ten thousands
6. ones
7. thousands
8. ten thousands
9. hundreds
10. tens
11. hundred thousands
12. ten thousands

Practice Page 5:

80	40	70
400	300	700
5,000	90,000	35,580

Practice Page 6:

1.

Number	Nearest 10	Nearest 100
617	620	600
1,862	1,860	1,900
4,345	4,350	4,300
89,083	89,080	89,100

2. (Top to bottom) 1,000; 10,000; 90,000; 400,000; 900; 300,000

3. (Top to bottom) 900,000; 192,870; 810,000; 400,000; 922,000; 240,000

Practice Page 7:

crab cakes

C-842, N-293, K-769, B-525, R-636, T-971, E-537, A-328, S-450, P-792, J-387, F-614

Practice Page 8:

1,059	1,097	1,199
8,905	11,793	10,011
1,282	21,357	10,965

Practice Page 9:

1. (Left to right) 10,426; 1,047; 619; 8,214; 5,963; 1,074; 10,426 + 619 = 11,045

2. (Left to right) 8,807; 93,363; 71,362; 493,581; 9,361; 691,858

Practice Page 10:

Hi honey, I'm hair.

O-398, N-263, E-185, L-474, D-256, Y-647, I-739, A-498, H-532, M-159, R-326, U-565

Practice Page 11:

509	209	693
186	368	158
1,567	257	759

Practice Page 12:

1. 4,337	7. 181
2. 363	8. 533
3. 1,472	9. 2,391
4. 40,945	10. 7,341
5. 45,313	11. 63,377
6. 1,115	12. 88,268

Practice Page 13:

1. 15 eggs
2. 13 boats

Practice Page 14:

1. $6 \times 5 = 30$; $3 \times 10 = 30$; $30 = 30$
2. $7 \times 9 = 63$; $11 \times 6 = 66$; $63 < 66$
3. $6 \times 7 = 42$; $5 \times 8 = 40$; $42 > 40$
4. $7 \times 5 = 35$; $6 \times 6 = 36$; $35 < 36$
5. $5 \times 5 = 25$; $8 \times 3 = 24$; $25 > 24$
6. $2 \times 9 = 18$; $6 \times 3 = 18$; $18 = 18$
7. $7 \times 2 = 14$; $4 \times 4 = 16$; $14 < 16$
8. $12 \times 7 = 84$; $9 \times 9 = 81$; $84 > 81$

Practice Page 15:

1. 120	13. 48,000
2. 350	14. 28,000
3. 2,100	15. 18,000
4. 200	16. 24,000
5. 1,200	17. 15,000
6. 4,800	18. 56,000
7. 240	19. 24,000
8. 3,000	20. 72,000
9. 1,800	21. 48,000
10. 180	22. 81,000
11. 2,000	23. 12,000
12. 4,200	24. 100,000

Practice Page 16:

300	800	1,500
460	310	720
1,170	7,533	3,792

Practice Page 17:
Answers will vary. Check students' work.

Practice Page 18:
1. (Left to right) 180; 392; 1,588; 4,512; 4,896; <u>624</u>; 1,866; <u>301</u>; 3,355
2. (Left to right) 726; 253; 504; 4,752; <u>2,496</u>; 2,175; <u>2,604</u>; 3,652

Practice Page 19:
1. 120 toes
2. 960 legs
3. 16 toes
4. 1,128 legs
5. 80 toes
6. 18 toes
BONUS!—2 owls

Practice Page 20:
For each tower, the student should circle the blocks with the quotients that are shown here in bold.

12: 12)$\overline{144}$ = **12**; 5)$\overline{60}$ = **12**; 12)$\overline{12}$ = **1**; 11)$\overline{132}$ = **12**; 4)$\overline{44}$ = **11**

8: 3)$\overline{24}$ = **8**; 9)$\overline{63}$ = 7; 4)$\overline{36}$ = 9; 6)$\overline{48}$ = **8**; 12)$\overline{84}$ = 7

4: 5)$\overline{35}$ = 7; 8)$\overline{32}$ = **4**; 10)$\overline{40}$ = **4**; 12)$\overline{48}$ = **4**; 2)$\overline{8}$ = **4**

9: 9)$\overline{81}$ = **9**; 11)$\overline{77}$ = 7; 8)$\overline{72}$ = **9**; 3)$\overline{27}$ = **9**; 12)$\overline{108}$ = **9**

7: 6)$\overline{42}$ = **7**; 7)$\overline{49}$ = **7**; 2)$\overline{14}$ = **7**; 8)$\overline{64}$ = 8; 3)$\overline{21}$ = **7**

Practice Page 21:

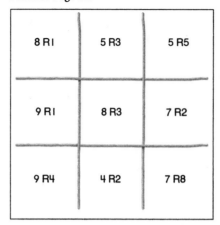

8 R1	5 R3	5 R5
9 R1	8 R3	7 R2
9 R4	4 R2	7 R8

Practice Page 22:

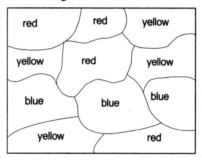

red	red	yellow
yellow	red	yellow
blue	blue	blue
yellow		red

Practice Page 23:

21	42	11
36	82	53
192	178	92

Practice Page 24:
Estimates may vary; sample estimates:

1. 5
2. 7
3. 40
4. 60
5. 100
6. 60
7. 50
8. 400
9. 400
10. 70
11. 4
12. 70
13. 80
14. 50
15. 700
16. 900
17. 600
18. 700

Practice Page 25:
Answers will vary. Check students' work.

Practice Page 26:
1. 25 people
2. 45 people

Practice Page 27:

$5 each	32 baseball cards	45 sticks of gum
12 stickers	51 minutes	24 cookies
42 weeks	504 hours	11,772 miles

Practice Page 28:
Answers will vary. Check students' work.

Practice Page 29:
1. 85 seats
2. $336,600

Practice Page 30:
1. 5 ×
2. 11 +
3. 9 ×
4. 28 −
5. 17 +
6. 39 −
7. 7 ×
8. 4 ×
9. 6 +
10. 6 ×

Practice Page 31:

$6.75	10 fish	2 kids
14 points	2 minutes	$4.50
24 points	10,000 people	$125,000

Practice Page 32:
1. 144
2. 210; 3.5
3. 607
4. 1,200; 28,800
5. 4,167; 69

Practice Page 33:
1. 1 and 18, 2 and 9, 3 and 6
2. 1 and 24, 2 and 12, 3 and 8, 4 and 6
3. 1 and 52, 2 and 26, 4 and 13
4. 1 and 64, 2 and 32, 4 and 16, 8 and 8
5. 1 and 72, 2 and 36, 3 and 24, 4 and 18, 6 and 12, 8 and 9
6. 1 and 96, 2 and 48, 3 and 32, 4 and 24, 6 and 16, 8 and 12

Practice Page 34:
1. Multiples of 3 only—3, 6, 9, 12, 18, 21, 24, 27, 33, 36, 39, 42, 48; multiples of 5 only—5, 10, 20, 25, 35, 40, 50; both—15, 30, 45
2. Multiples of 4 only—4, 8, 16, 20, 28, 32, 40, 44; multiples of 6 only—6, 18, 30, 42; both—12, 24, 36, 48

Practice Page 35:

10 (add 2 to the previous number)	13 (add 3 to the previous number)	25 (subtract 5 from the previous number)
25, 24, 27 (add 3 to the previous number; subtract 1 from the total)	105, 73, 9 (subtract 2, then 4, then 8, then 16, and so on; the number subtracted from each number is 2 times the number that was subtracted from the previous number)	8,100, 8,050, 8,025 (subtract 800, then 400, then 200, and so on; the number subtracted from each number is ½ the number subtracted from the previous number)
Sunday (add 2 days to the previous day of the week)	April 2 (add 1 week to the previous date)	6:06 (add 14 minutes to the previous time)

Practice Page 36:
1. CDE, EFG
2. 26, 55
3. ✖, ▲▲▲▲
4. 66, 44
5. k, o
6. ➔, ⬆
7. x, t, p
8. B, W, F

BONUS!—Answers will vary.

Practice Page 37:
Iguanodon
1. 9, 11, 13
2. 32, 64, 128
3. 20, 15, 9
4. 21, 26, 31
5. 17, 22, 28
6. 9, 3, 1
7. ●●●, ★★★, ●●●●
8. ★★★●●●, ★★★★●●●, ★★★★●●●●
9. ★★★, ★★★●●●, ★★★★

Practice Page 38:
Answers will vary. Check students' work.

Practice Page 39:

Town hall	Soccer field	Fruit stand
(1,8)	(7,1)	Grocery store
10 minutes	35 minutes	6 routes

Practice Page 40:
arthropods
1. A
2. R
3. T
4. H
5. R
6. O
7. P
8. O
9. D
10. S

Practice Page 41:
1. $54 \div n = 9$; 6
2. $n \div 3 = 129$; 387
3. $129 \div n = 3$; 42
4. $n \div 9 = 66$; 594
5. $n \times 15 = 1{,}950$; 130

Practice Page 42:
1. $n + 435 = 1{,}966$; 1,531
2. $625 - n = 52$; 573
3. $1{,}000 \times n = 0$; 0
4. $n \div 48 = 64$; 3,072
5. $7 \times n = 448$; 64
6. $151 \times n = 1{,}812$; 12
7. $396 \div n = 11$; 36
8. $2{,}005 \div n = 401$; 5

Practice Page 43:
Answers will vary. Check students' work.

Practice Page 44:
Cheer up!
R-$\frac{1}{3}$, U-$\frac{3}{4}$, C-$\frac{1}{2}$, E-$\frac{5}{6}$, M-$\frac{5}{7}$, N-$\frac{6}{10}$, W-$\frac{2}{5}$, H-$\frac{7}{8}$, K-$\frac{1}{4}$, P-$\frac{4}{6}$

Practice Page 45:
1. $\frac{7}{9}$
2. $\frac{1}{9}$
3. $\frac{6}{9}$, or $\frac{2}{3}$
4. $\frac{4}{9}$
5. $\frac{5}{9}$
6. $\frac{1}{4}$
7. $\frac{3}{5}$
8. $\frac{1}{3}$

BONUS!—3

Practice Page 46:

2	4	2
no	yes	no
$\frac{8}{12}$	$\frac{45}{81}$	$\frac{6}{8}$

Practice Page 47:
in meteor showers
M-2, O-3, S-6, E-4, A-9, I-5, H-11, T-8, R-30, N-12, G-7, W-10

Practice Page 48:
St. Lawrence Seaway
1. R, $\frac{18}{20}$
2. E, $\frac{12}{15}$
3. W, $\frac{6}{9}$
4. A, $\frac{12}{27}$
5. L, $\frac{15}{20}$
6. S, $\frac{10}{25}$
7. E, $\frac{15}{24}$
8. N, $\frac{3}{18}$
9. W, $\frac{12}{32}$
10. T, $\frac{18}{21}$
11. Y, $\frac{15}{18}$
12. E, $\frac{10}{14}$
13. A, $\frac{10}{24}$
14. C, $\frac{50}{100}$
15. A, $\frac{21}{30}$
16. S, $\frac{21}{24}$

Practice Page 49:

2	4	5
$\frac{3}{4}$	$\frac{1}{3}$	$\frac{3}{5}$
$\frac{2}{9}$	$\frac{2}{7}$	$\frac{2}{5}$

Practice Page 50:
a spot remover
S-1/3, R-5/6, V-3/4, O-2/3, E-7/8, L-3/5, T-1/9, B-7/9, C-7/10, M-1/8, P-1/4, A-5/7

Practice Page 51:
seismosaurus

1. S, 3/4	**7.** S, 3/4
2. A, 3/8	**8.** E, 4/11
3. I, 2/5	**9.** U, 3/7
4. S, 3/4	**10.** M, 5/6
5. R, 7/9	**11.** U, 3/7
6. O, 5/12	**12.** S, 3/4

Practice Page 52:
Answers will vary. Check students' work.

Practice Page 53:
I. Ben Stung
B-3/15, U-1/5, S-4/6, E-2/3, G-15/30, N-1/2, T-6/8, I-3/4

Practice Page 54:

<	=	>
=	<	>
2/3, 1/3, 1/6	3/4, 5/8, 3/8, 1/4	5/6, 4/6, 3/6, 7/12

Practice Page 55:
They raise a racket.
T-1/2, A-1/3, Y-1/4, H-1/8, K-4/5, E-2/3, X-3/4, S-3/5, I-5/8, P-6/12, C-3/8, R-2/6

Practice Page 56:
Virginia Dare

1. V, 1/4	7. I, 5/8
2. I, 3/5	8. A, 1/12
3. R, 3/4	9. D, 9/12
4. G, 1/7	10. A, 4/11
5. I, 15/25	11. R, 7/10
6. N, 7/8	12. E, 5/9

Practice Page 57:
a ducks-edo
R-3/4, A-11/12, S-4/5, D-5/6, O-5/8, L-7/9, C-5/7, N-10/11, T-6/8, K-6/7, E-9/10, U-2/3

Practice Page 58:
Answers will vary. Check students' work.

Practice Page 59:

1	1/2	1/10
3/4	1/2	1/2 of the songs
2/3	1/4	3/4 of her birthday money

Practice Page 60:
bristlecone pine

O. 3/5	**I.** 1/2
S. 1 1/3	**T.** 4/9
V. 1 1/6	**B.** 3/4
R. 5/7	**L.** 1/3
H. 1 2/3	**Y.** 1
P. 1 3/7	**N.** 5/6
M. 1/4	**E.** 2/3
C. 1 1/2	

Practice Page 61:
He needed a multi-plier.
M-2/4, D-1/8, E-3/6, R-7/12, A-5/9, T-2/5, P-3/7, N-4/11, U-8/14, L-6/10, I-9/15, H-1/3

Practice Page 62:
Answers will vary. Check students' work.

Practice Page 63:

1 5/8	1 1/6	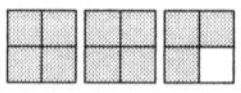
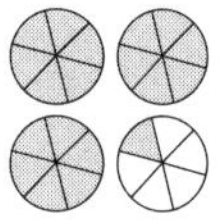	11 slices	1 3/5
2 1/3	5/2	yes

Practice Page 64:
a giant fungus

1. A, 2 2/3	**7.** F, 2 1/3
2. G, 5 2/5	**8.** U, 5 1/2
3. N, 3 3/7	**9.** I, 4 1/4
4. A, 4 2/3	**10.** G, 9 1/2
5. N, 5 1/3	**11.** U, 1 7/12
6. S, 9 1/3	**12.** T, 2 1/5

Practice Page 65:
a monkey wrench
E-10, H-1 2/3, K-1 5/6, Y-1, C-8, M-3 3/4, W-8 1/2, R-3, T-2 3/7, N-3 2/3, A-6, O-1 7/8

Practice Page 66:
Leif Ericsson

C. 1 2/7	**S.** 3 1/4
M. 6 1/2	**O.** 6 3/5
H. 11 1/6	**F.** 4 1/3
I. 4 2/3	**D.** 9 1/2
R. 2 3/4	**W.** 3 3/7
E. 7 3/5	**N.** 6
J. 2 5/6	**L.** 2 5/7
A. 7	

Practice Page 67:

5	12	20
15	9	20
6 candies	4 days	20 games

Practice Page 68:
It wooden go.
S-2, A-2 6/7, T-1/3, R-1 1/2, O-3 3/7, N-3/5, W-4 2/3, I-3 1/3, G-2 1/4, D-1 2/5, E-12, L-6 2/9

Practice Page 69:
Answers will vary. Check students' work.

Practice Page 70:
on strike
N-5 hundredths, I-0 hundredths, Y-4 ones, R-1 tenth, O-6 ones, T-9 hundredths, S-2 ones, E-7 tenths, K-8 tenths

Practice Page 71:
1. 0.3
2. 0.6
3. 0.26
4. 0.47
5. (Left to right) 0.3; 0.07; 0.62; 0.16; 0.9; 0.01

Practice Page 72:

0.6	0.3	1.5
0.21	0.72	1.15
5.5, 4.56, 5.6, 5.65	10.04, 10.14, 10.3, 10.34, 10.4, 10.43	4.5, 4.58, 4.8, 4.81, 4.85, 4.9

Practice Page 73:
Answers will vary. Check students' work.

Practice Page 74:
1. 1.2, 1.5, 1.6, 1.9
2. 6.1, 6.4, 6.7, 6.8
3. 1.02, 1.05, 1.06, 1.92
4. 4.47, 6.14, 6.43, 6.73
5. 10.9, 10.6, 10.1, 0.4
6. 12.8, 12.7, 12.3, 11.9
7. 10.91, 10.06, 10.01, 9.99
8. 12.37, 12.23, 11.23, 10.16

Practice Page 75:
herpetologists

1. E, $\frac{1}{10}$
2. I, $1\frac{29}{100}$
3. R, $\frac{1}{5}$
4. O, $6\frac{7}{10}$
5. O, $\frac{9}{100}$
6. H, $5\frac{3}{4}$
7. S, $\frac{1}{2}$
8. L, $4\frac{7}{10}$
9. E, $\frac{59}{100}$
10. T, $5\frac{9}{20}$
11. S, $\frac{1}{20}$
12. P, $\frac{22}{25}$
13. T, $\frac{3}{100}$
14. G, $\frac{11}{50}$

Practice Page 76:
a comedi-hen
I-.34, F-.1, C-.2, A-.17, E-.61, O-.4, H-.5, M-.01, D-.8, G-.99, K-.05, N-.74

Practice Page 77:
1. (Left to right) 0.4; 0.25; 1.5; 3.9; 2.75; 1.75; 7.25; 0.7; 5.8; 0.24; 11.03; 20.15
2. (Left to right) $\frac{35}{100}$; $4\frac{6}{10}$; $3\frac{75}{100}$; $\frac{17}{100}$; $5\frac{97}{100}$; $4\frac{63}{100}$; $\frac{85}{100}$; $60\frac{5}{10}$; $99\frac{99}{100}$; $2\frac{2}{100}$; $\frac{7}{100}$; $75\frac{75}{100}$

Practice Page 78:
She was a good batter.
S-3.0, T-8.1, J-4.60, G-5.55, H-1.5, B-21.211, A-7.11, W-6.1, D-11.8, E-7.65, R-9.7, O-2.6

Practice Page 79:
Answers will vary. Check students' work.

Practice Page 80:
1.

0	.1	0.2	.3	.4	0.5	.6	.7	.8	0.9	1
$\frac{0}{10}$	$\frac{1}{10}$	$\frac{2}{10}$	$\frac{3}{10}$	$\frac{4}{10}$	$\frac{5}{10}$	$\frac{6}{10}$	$\frac{7}{10}$	$\frac{8}{10}$	$\frac{9}{10}$	$\frac{10}{10}$

2. Sample answers: (Left to right) 2.1, 2.2, 2.3; 8.5, 8.3, 8.1; 12.5, 12.6, 12.7; 79.9, 79.8, 79.7; 5.6, 5.7, 5.8; 3.17, 3.16, 3.15
3. 8.05; 8.5; 3.75; 3.97

Practice Page 81:
1. 1 foot
2. 5 miles
3. 10 pounds
4. 5 inches
5. 2 pounds
6. 7 centimeters
7. 1 cup
8. 3 feet
9. 90°F
10. 28°F

Practice Page 82:
credit card
1. E
2. A
3. I
4. C
5. E
6. R
7. T
8. R

Practice Page 83:

48	60	38
6	14	5,280
3,520	5,580	1 mile, 1,020 feet

Practice Page 84:
1. 1,140 feet
2. 10

Practice Page 85:

6:15 A.M.	22 minutes	18 minutes late
9:35 A.M.	45 minutes (:45)	6 hours, 30 minutes (6:30)
1 hour, 27 minutes (1:27)	2 hours, 25 minutes (2:25)	11 hours, 48 minutes (11:48)

Practice Page 86:
1. 12:40 P.M.
2. 2.31 seconds
3. 86,400 seconds
4. 375 minutes, or 6 hours 15 minutes

Practice Page 87:
1. 10
2. 12 cups

Practice Page 88:
1. 2.5 grams
2. 40 bags
3. 37.5 pounds
4. 264 pounds

Practice Page 89:
1. $8.65
2. $20.59
3. $40.30
4. $41.80
5. $49.48
6. $40.95

Practice Page 90:

$8.00	$5.00	$6.50
$5.98	$7.48	$5.00
$15.47	$19.47	$30.92

Practice Page 91:
1. $12.98; $7.02; 1 $5 bill, 2 $1 bills, 2 pennies
2. $23.14; $26.86; 1 $20 bill, 1 $5 bill, 1 $1 bill, 3 quarters, 1 dime, and 1 penny (Students might suggest 1 half-dollar and 1 quarter rather than 3 quarters.)
3. $21.42; $8.58; 1 $5 bill, 3 $1 bills, 2 quarters (or 1 half-dollar), 1 nickel, 3 pennies

Practice Page 92:
1. 44 square units
2. 2,106 square feet
3. 80 feet
4. 54 meters

Practice Page 93:
1. 384 feet; 48; $767.52
2. 6,272 square feet; 224 square feet; 6,048 square feet; 2,016 square feet; 8,064 square feet
3. 192 square feet; 576 flowers; 56 feet

Practice Page 94:
1. 30 **2.** 9 **3.** 4 hours **4.** 3 **5.** 10

Practice Page 95:

February	decrease	20 inches
40 inches	5 inches	decreased
15 inches less	February	March

Practice Page 96:
1. June; 25
2. February; 2
3. February–March, March–April, April–May
4. July–August, August–September, September–October
5. 22; 15; 7
6. June and July
7. winter
8. Answers may vary; a possible answer follows: The sales of surfboards increase from February to June. Sales decrease from June to November, then increase slightly for December. Sales increase in anticipation of summer and the December gift-giving season.

Practice Page 97:
1. 12 fright wigs
2. wind-up mice
3. squirt pens
4. 40
5. rubber snakes
6. 14
BONUS!—80

Practice Page 98:

ray	line segment	line
intersecting	parallel	intersecting
parallel	perpendicular	perpendicular

Practice Page 99:
1. greater than
2. less than
3. less than
4. right angle
5. acute angle
6. obtuse angle
7. acute triangle
8. right triangle
9. obtuse triangle

Practice Page 100:
1. Check that students' drawings are symmetrical.
2. Check that students' drawings are symmetrical.